# The Italian Cartel

*"There are rules to partnerships"*

*Created and Written By*

Giancarlo Giacobbone

# Characters and families:

# The Italian Mob

Don Gian Barone- *(Italian Mob boss of US 5 families)*

Tony *(Two times)* DiMaggio- *(Don Gian #2 Capo)*

Joey Barone– *(Raised by Don Gian as an orphan)*

Frankie Barone- *(Don Gian son)*

Josephine *(late wife of Don Gian and sister to Armando Bimino)*

## 5 Families

-Bimino Family *(Chicago)*

- Armando Bimino *(head of the house, Don Gian's brother-in-law)*
- Angelo Bimino *(son)*

-Stelleti family- *(Cali)*

- Johnny Stelleti *(head of house, Don Gian's first cousin)*

-Ranile family *(FL)*

- Vinny Ranile *(Head of house, longtime friend)*

-Lentucci Family *(Texas)*

- Joe Lentucci- *(Head of house longtime friend)*

**Top Italian Family in Napoli** *(Marco and Sylvester, brothers of The Scopa Family)*

Gino- *(mob employee- manages café di Napoli)*

Charlie- *(mob employee)*

Vincenzo- *(Family doctor)*

Sal Domani- *(Joey's friend, construction business)*

Silvestro Pinto- *(Lawyer)*

## The Mexican Cartel

Angela Felix- *(Mexican cartel boss in the US)*

Eduardo Felix- *(Angela's late husband)*

Daniel Felix-*(Angela's son)*

Veronica Felix- *(Daniel Felix's wife)*

Maria Felix – *(Angela Felix's daughter)*

Miquel Suarez- *(Maria Felix's husband)*

José Méndez – *(Ángela Félix #2)*

Luis- *(cartel employee)*

Joaquin twin, Santiago and Xavier

**Top Cartel Boss in Mexico** *(Jesus, The Mendoza family)*

Maya Mendoza- *(Jesus Daughter)*

## Police

Matteo- *(NYPD)*

Detective Dave Morrow- *(FBI Agent)*

Lorenzo Pani- *(FBI Agent)*

Dedicated to my loving father,
Antonio Giacobbone.


*(Frank Sinatra's "The Way You Look Tonight" echoes through a house to a bathroom nestled in the back. A 9mm handgun sits upon the Tub; a woman sits sobbing with tears in her eyes. A sudden knock at the door. Bang! It fires and floats down upon the bathroom floor. It begins to spin until the floor tile cracks, slows it down, and stops... and points back at you.)*

# Table of Contents

# Chapter 1

# "College"18  Years later…

*It's a hot, muggy day in the summer of 2010 in queens, NY. The ice cream truck rings its bell as kids play in the water of open fire hydrants. Old men sit playing chess in the park. It's a quiet and free neighborhood watched over by generations of Italian immigrants who migrated to this country in search of a new life.*

## <u>EXT Café Di Napoli In Middle Village NY</u>

*(Two people in front of a café called café di Napoli are having a playful argument over an ideal woman)*

Frankie- Joey, you don't understand you need a nice Italian woman who can cook and greets you with a kiss and a nice pear-shaped ass as soon as you walk through the door.

Joey-I disagree.. I don't care if she can cook or not; I'll order a pizza from Andrews with a Hello motor boat… Charlie has that pear-shaped ass you like so much, why don't you talk to him.

Frankie- That's like me saying you want to motorboat Gino, gets the fuck out of here with that.

*(Enter Tony two times, DiMaggio)*

Tony-Frankie, Your dad wants a word with you, you.

Frankie- I didn't catch that; what did you say?

Tony- Get the fuck in there before I back slap you, you.

Joey- Hey T, what are you going to do again?

Tony- you two cock smokers are funny, aren't Ya, Ya.

Joey- no, just Frankie, but I only tell him he's funny one time, one time …. *(Laughing)*

*(Tony smacks Joey upside the head)*

Joey- ahh Testa di minchia ! *(Dickhead)* Does Don need me also?

Tony- No, Just Frankie, Frankie.

Frankie-Just me, Joe, just me…. *(Laughing)* Get a pie from Andrews; I'll only be a minute. Maybe you'll find those perfect double D's on your way there. Tell Andrew I said he's a braciola.

*(Joey laughs as he walks away as Frankie enters the cafe)*

*(Two Men in an El Camino pull up and begin to enter a Mexican restaurant across the street called Viva Mexicana. One of the men begins to eye Joey. Joey, aware, begins staring him down and yells toward him.)*

Joey- You got a problem, Daniel!?

Daniel- Fuck You Puto!

*(Joey starts to walk toward Daniel cursing, while Tony is still outside and runs toward Joey to stop him)*

Tony- Joey, Joey!

Joey- He's got a problem with me, T, and I want to know what it is…!?

Tony- Just let it go, go. We need to mind our business, you understand? Pensa Sempre la famiglia, famiglia. *(Always think of the family)*

*(Joey begins to calm down)*

Joey-ok T, out of respect for the family, I will but fuck that asshole! *(makes a middle finger gesture toward Daniel)*

*(Daniel makes one final stare and gestures back as he heads into the restaurant)*

## <u>INT Viva Mexicana Middle Village, NY</u>

Daniel- donde esta Ángela. *(where is Angela? he asks a worker)*

Restaurant Worker- En su oficina. *(In her office)*

*(They proceed to the back room)*

José- Hola jefe.

Ángela-Todo va según lo planeado José? *(all go as planned?)*

Jose, we dropped the product exactly where you asked us to.

Angela- Bueno.

Daniel- Who came to pick it up? I know it wasn't the Joaquin twins. Who is moving our product? We have been doing these same drops for two years now, but I never know who is on the other end of the pickup.

Angela- That is not your concern right now, hijo. *(Son)*

Daniel-Why must there always be secrets with you? Why can't you ever be honest?

Angela- When the time comes, I will tell you everything you will need to know, but as for now, do not ever question me again, you hear me!? *(Her voice beginning to get stern)*

Daniel- Just like you told me, my father died in a car accident on the way to the hospital when I was born, right? Fuck this shit!

*(Daniel, annoyed, storms out of the restaurant)*

## <u>INT  Café Di Napoli</u>

Frankie -Ciao papa, volevi vedermi? *(Hi dad, You wanted to see me?)*

Don Gian- Si frankie, vieni qui. *(Yes, Frankie, come here)* I need you to do something for me.

Frankie- What's that?

Don Gian- I need you to keep an eye on Joey.

Frankie- What do you mean to keep an eye on him?

Don Gian- You know he reacts on instinct, and that's not necessarily good noise. Make sure he doesn't do anything stupid.

Frankie I understand that he is always full of emotion, and it sometimes overtakes him. I will do my best.

Don Gian –No, your best is not good enough; I need you to DO! Cazzo!

Frankie- OK, I will, I promise.

Don Gian-Bene, Tony must go pick something up. I want you to go with him.

Frankie- are you finally going to let me in?

Don Gian-*(shouts)* Charlie! vai a prendere Tony e digli di venire qui. (get tony and tell him to come here)

Charlie- Ok, lo faro.

*(Charlie exits and proceeds to go find Tony outside)*

Frankie-Are you going to tell me what we are picking up?

*(Don ignores his son's questions, and then Tony enters)*

Tony- Si capo, Capo? *(Yes boss, yes boss?)*

Don Gian- Take Frankie to Astoria with you

Tony- Va bene, bene

Don Gian- listen to Tony, and whatever he tells you to do, you do. You got me? And don't ask questions, understand me?

Frankie- *(feeling confused)* but …

Don Gian – *(cuts him off)* AH AH AA! Just keep it to yourself for now. We will talk more soon, lo prometto. *(I promise)*

## <u>INT Andrews Pizzeria in Middle Village, NY</u>

Joey – Riccione. *(faggot)*

Andrew – Oh banana que fai. (hey, banana, what are you doing?)

Joey- cosa pensi che voglia? Una pizza stronzo. Come sta a famiglia? *(What do you think I want? A pizza stupid, how's the family)*

Andrew- They are good; Michelle just had a little girl last week.

Joey- That's great. I didn't even know she was pregnant.

Andrew- She lives out on the island. She hardly comes around as much.

Joey- Congratulations! Wish her my best. You guys are closed next week right?

Andrew- 4th of July week every year...

Joey- Why don't you let me run things while you're on vacation? It would be like you never closed.

Andrew- I appreciate the suggestion, but I'm going to leave things this way. I need a week when I don't have to worry about this place.

Joey- You know I could make a good pie.

Andrew- I know you can, but it's been five years since you worked here. Why don't you start applying for college and think about what career you want to pursue?

Joey- I didn't even want to finish high school. I only did it because Don wanted me to, but now that I'm almost 18, I want to enter the family business.

Andrew – no disrespect to you or the **Barone's**, but you have much more potential than settling with the family business. You are a smart kid.

Joey- You know you are like family to me, Andrew, but I'm gonna do what I'm gonna do.

Andrew- Here's your pie, Banana, just think about it...

Joey- Grazie! Ciao braciole.

## INT Woods Hotel in Queens, NY

*(Knocking at the door)*

Verónica Félix- - Quién es? *(who is it?)*

Joey- It's your bright and shining armor.

*(She opens the door)*

Verónica Félix- Where you been? I'm hungry.

Joey- I had to make sure Daniel didn't follow me. I saw him by the café. So? You're hungry, huh? *(He grabs Veronica and throws her on the bed as the door closes)*

## INT Maria's Beauty Salon In Ridgewood Queens

Maria Felix Suarez- Did you check the receipts from yesterday?

Miquel Suarez- Yes, I told you I did.

Maria- They all match up.

Miquel- All is in order.

Maria  You know why I keep asking you, right?

Miquel- Your mother will have my head.

Maria- She has never been that fond of you, and to include you in this business, she expects nothing but perfection from you.

Miquel- I still don't understand what I ever did to her.

María- Nena tu colombiana. *(Babe, you're Columbian)* She hates Columbians.

Miquel- I may be Columbian, but I'm on your side you know.

Maria-It doesn't matter what I think, and yes, you are on my side. Mi Amor.

*(They kiss)*

## **INT Woods Hotel**

Joey- There's nothing like Andrews pizza after playing your violin.

Veronica- After? You tried during… Sometimes, I think you like your pizza more than you like me.

Joey- I think they go hand in hand.

*(Veronica slaps Joey jokingly)*

Veronica - You can't have your cake and eat it too.

Joey - Of course I can—some people like fudge, some like strawberries. I like pizza.

Veronica – You're such a dick.

Joey- Yes, but you like this dick. *(Points to his privates)*

*(He jumps on top and kisses Veronica)*

Veronica- I have to go. I'm sure Daniel is calling me off the hook, and I have my phone shut off.

Joey- Don't you think that's a bad idea?

Veronica- No, he knows my phone always dies because I forget to charge it, and it's a piece of Crap.  I'll go to Su's salon and get my nails done to show him where I've been.

Joey- When are you going to leave him?

Veronica- You know I can't

Joey- Yes, you can.

Veronica- You can say that because your father…

*(He cuts her off)*

Joey- He's not really my father.

Veronica- OK, your adopted father who raised you is giving you options in life.

Joey- The only option I prefer is to prove to him that I belong. Whatever they want me to do, I will, even if it means killing somebody.

Veronica- Stop it! You're not that kind of person, and you know it. You're better than that. Go make something of yourself. Go to college; take a step toward your future. You know this could never be more than what it is.

Joey- It can be if you tried.

Veronica – I can't, I have to go.

*(She kisses Joey and leaves)*

## <u>EXT Warehouse in Astoria Queens</u>

Tony- Bring the car around to the loading dock, dock

Frankie- Ok T.

*(Tony opens the gates from inside of the warehouse)*

Frankie- Listen, T I'm not fucking with you here, but I'm kind of curious to know. Why do you repeat yourself? Is it a twitch or something?

Tony- Accident. a long time ago, ago.

Frankie- You got hit by a car or something?

Tony- No, I got shot in the head, head.

*(Frankie pauses)*

Frankie-Oh... sorry

Tony- Now, do us both a favor and open the back, back.

*(Tony loads about four pallets with a lift gate into the truck)*

Frankie- What's in the pallets T?

*(Tony stares at Frankie)*

Frankie- *(holds his hands up)* Okay, okay, no questions. I got it.

*(After the truck is loaded and doors are secured with zip ties, they leave)*

## **INT New Jersey Warehouse In Secaucus, NJ**

Don Gian Barone- Benvenuto mia famiglia, è passato molto tempo. *(hello my family it's been a long time)*

*(They greet with kisses on the cheeks. We see a big round table with five chairs in the middle of the warehouse)*

Don Gian- Accomodiamoci. *(have a seat)*

Johnny Stelleti- Cugino, è il prodotto in arrivo? *(Cousin, is the product on the way?)*

Don Gian- Sì tra poco, Frankie e Tony stanno arrivando. *(Yes, in a little while, Frankie and Tony are arriving soon)*

Vinny Ranile- Frankie? Lui sa? *(frankie knows?)*

Don Gian-Un poco a la volta. *(A little at a time)*

Joe Ientucci- E Bimino? *(And Bimino?)*

Don Gian-che ne pensi di loro. *(What about them?)*

Johnny Stelleti- Continuano a fare domande. *(They continue to ask questions)*

Don Gian- Ci preoccuperemo di loro quando il momento arriva,nel Frattempo un poco alla Volta per Frankie, ok... *(We will worry about them when the time comes; in the meantime a little at a time for Frankie, ok.. ))*

Joe Lentucci-non vedo frankie da anni. *(I haven't seen Frankie in years)* <u>sta bene?</u> *( is he well?*

Don Gian - tutti cresciuto *(all grown up)*

Vinny Ranile- 18 right?

Don Gian –diciannove. *(19)*

Johnny stelleti- Madonna Mia, 19? *(Oh my god, 19?)*

*(The gates of the warehouse open, and we see Frankie and Tony have arrived)*

Don Gian- Eccolo. *(Here he is)*

Frankie- Oh shit! Is this a party? Ciao tutti, come state? *(Hello all, how are you?)* Joe, are you still wearing ugly cowboy boots and riding your horses in Texas?

Joe Lentucci- *(laughing)* If brains were dynamite, you wouldn't have enough to blow your nose. Come here.

*(They embrace in a hug)*

Frankie- I haven't seen you guys in years. What's going on?

Don Gian- Tony, bring the pallets.

*(Tony goes and loads pallets onto the life gate and brings each in one by one)*

Don Gian-Frankie, what you see and what you hear here today remains with the people in this room. Do you understand me?

Frankie- Si. *(Yes)*

*(Don Nods at Tony)*

*(Tony opens the pallet, and to Frankie's surprise, there are blocks of cocaine)*

Frankie-Is that cocaine? I thought we owned the race tracks/racketeering, etc. I did not know we were in the drug business.

Johnny Stelleti- Cuz, it is very important that this information stays with the people here. No one else knows, not the Bimino family and certainly not the Scopa family.

Frankie- But I don't understand why not the Bimino family. "I haven't seen them since the 10-year anniversary of my mother's death".

Don Gian- Frankie, Come with me.

*(They walk into the back office)*

Don Gian- Frankie, if people were to find out what we are doing, it would be really bad for us. The Scopa family doesn't take this stuff lightly. They did not want us to get involved in the drug business. Ho ignorato la loro richiesta *(I ignored their request),* you understand what that means, right?

Frankie- Can I ask who we get it from?

Don Gian- The Viva Mexicana cartel.

Frankie- What!? Seriously? Is that why you allow them to be right across the street? You know Joey hates them, right, especially Daniel.

Don Gian- That is exactly why you cannot tell him or anyone else. You wanted this, right?

Frankie- Yes, of course.

Don Gian- Then you must keep this to yourself, or else there could be consequences. posso fidarmi di te figlio? *(Can I trust you son?)*

Frankie- Si, papa.

Don Gian-Tony ti dira quello che devi sapere  *(tony   will tell you what you need to know)*

## <u>INT Daniel and Veronica Home in Forest Hills, Queens, NY</u>

*(Veronica arrives home to find Daniel drinking tequila on the couch with Luis)*

Daniel- Where the fuck have you been?

Veronica- I went to the salon to do my nails and get a Pedi.

Daniel- That's funny, considering I spoke to my sister Maria, and she has not seen or spoken to you all day. Both your phones are always off, and now you're going to fucking lie to me!?

Veronica -I did not go to Maria's shop; I went to the Chinese one around the corner. They do better work than your sister's money laundering salon.

Daniel- Cállate! *(Shut up)* Let me see your fucking nails.

*(Veronica shows Daniel, and to his surprise, they look like they were just done)*

Veronica- You see all dollied up… *(Smiling)*

Daniel- I want your phones charged 24/7. If it goes to even 20%, I want you to find a fucking outlet and charge the fucking thing, you hear me?!

Veronica- Okay, okay. *(she walks into the back bedroom)*

*(Daniel turns to Luis)*

Daniel- Seguirla. *(follow her)*

Luis- Bueno. *(ok)*

## **<u>INT Café Di Napoli</u>**

Joey- Gino, don't you get tired of being here all fucking day? That would drive me insane. But I guess that makes sense for you since you eat everything, you fat bastard.

Gino- your here all fucking day too; why don't you go get a job or go put your dick in something.

Joey- I already did, but the pie got stale really quickly.

Gino- Stronzo sai. *(stupid you are)*

Joey- Hey, you seen Frankie around? I hadn't seen him all day, and he hasn't answered his phone.

Gino- I think he took a ride with Tony.

Joey- With T? Where to?

Gino- Che Cazzo ne so *(what the fuck do I know)* I'm here all day remember?

*(Joey takes a second to mull over why Frankie is out with Tony when his phone rings)*

Joey- Yah?

*(You don't hear the other end of that conversation, but the conversation continues)*

Joey- Tonight?  8, ok, see you then.

*(As Joey hangs up, he sees a car pull up, and Frankie comes out)*

Joey- Hey, braciole, where have you been all day? Repeating yourself with T. You guys should start a game show called Double Dipping with T bags.

Frankie- *(laughing)*You never run out, do you, Joe?

Joey- It's called sarcasm. I put that shit on everything.

Tony- Frank, I'll call you later, later.

Joey-Hey T, I know the best speech therapist. She has a cock and gives happy endings you interested?

Tony- One day, that mouth is gonna get you in trouble; Joey, be careful careful.

*(As Tony drives away, Joey yells)*

Joey –Yah, well, at least this mouth doesn't suck dick and repeat the gargling sound.

Frankie- Joe, what's your problem? Why are you being an extra ass to T?

Joey- What problem? I don't have a problem. Where have you been all day?

Frankie-Nowhere, T just took me to a couple of bookies and race tracks to show me some of the ropes.

Joey- "The Family business" I wonder why he didn't ask me to go. He knows how long I wanted to be a part of the business. I finished high school just like he asked. I guess it's only his true-born son who is allowed to enter the precious family business.

Frankie- You know that's not true, cuz, come on.  Why don't you go to college? Do..

*(Joey cuts him off)*

Joey- Again, with this fucking college, it's like a broken fucking record everywhere I go! College this and college that!  I don't want to go to college. Let me be my own man... Make my own fucking decisions for a change. Where's your father anyway?

Frankie- he's not here.

Joey- How the fuck…Do you know he's not here? You just got here!

Frankie- He called me and told me to meet him at the tracks.

Joey – At the tracks?

Frankie- At the tracks, at the tracks.

Joey-With the horses, with the horses?

*(Both laugh at the expense of Tony's speech problem)*

Frankie- Hey, by the way, where's the pie from Andrews?

Joey- You have been gone four fucking hours where you think it is.

Frankie- You fat bastard, you, and your pizza.

Joey- This fat bastard's gotta go

Frankie- Where you going? I thought we could get a couple beers tonight.

Joey- Not tonight. I'll call you later; answer your fucking phone, Frankie Smalls...

*(As he walks away, Frankie yells)*

Frankie- It's a girl, isn't it? puttana! *( whore)*

*(Joey grabs his crouch while smiling. Frankie stands there for a minute and mules over what his father told him)*

## <u>INT Frankie's Wash Brooklyn NY</u>

Don Gian,- you bring Frankie up to speed?

Tony- Si don, don.

Don Gian- Only about the business?

Tony- Of course, course.

Don Gian- Bene.

Tony- Joey seems more reckless lately, lately

Don Gian- We need to control him. I made him a promise that I will have to break, and it will go one of two ways. speriamo che capsica *( I hope he understands )*

## <u>EXT Woods Hotel</u>

*(Joey knocks on a door when a hand comes out and grabs him inside)*

Veronica- Were you followed?

Joey- No, why, what's going on?

Veronica- Daniel is getting suspicious and asking all sorts of questions.

Joey- I told you not to leave your phone off.

Veronica- I think we should take a break for a While, until things settle down with him.

Joey- No, we just have to take precautions.

Veronica- it's too dangerous, who knows what he would do.

*(Joey grabs her and tosses her on the bed)*

Joey- well, if that's the case, I guess we will have to make this time count for real.

*(Some time passes after another sexual encounter, and Joey is seen getting dressed)*

Joey-You know, I really like you.

Veronica- I really like you too.

Joey- I think I'm falling in love with you.

Veronica- Don't do that, Joe.

Joey- I'm just telling you how I feel. I will stay away, but I can't promise you for how long.

Veronica- Please Joe.

Joey-Ok, okay.

*(They kiss, and Joey leaves the hotel. Not to their knowledge, Luis is sitting in the car watching)*

*(Luis texts on his phone)*

Luis- I found her.

# Chapter 2
# "Ascolta" ("Listen")

<u>**INT Unknown Basement**</u>

*(Veronica is sitting tied, gagged, and her head covered with a blanket. Luis suddenly takes off the blanket, and she begins screaming at him through the gag)*

Veronica- GHahhhh….

*(Luis is just standing there like a Buckingham Palace Guard, not speaking, just staring straight and still. You can hear someone open the door, and it's Angela with Jose. She comes into view of Veronica and nods her head to Luis. He removes the gag. Veronica starts to plead)*

Veronica- Please don't tell Daniel! I made a mistake, please! I'm sorry…

*(Angela walks slowly toward a table behind Veronica.)*

Angela- Oh, don't you worry, he will not know a thing but…He's not the one you should be worried about.

*(She picks up some pliers while she walks in a circle around and into Veronica's view. She then begins to tell a story while Veronica sobs)*

Angela-You know, I once loved a man. I loved him more than anything in this world. I felt like I was living on a cloud at the time.

*(Walks closer to Veronica as Jose unties her, , and places her hands on another table directly in front of her)*

Angela-But at one point, he tried to take something from me, something that didn't belong to him.

Veronica- PLEASEE..

*(Angela Rips off one of Veronica's nails. She screams so loud that it echoes around the room, as the sound has nowhere to go)*

Veronica – Ahhhhhhhhhhhhhh! *(Screaming and pleading)*… NO… STOP… PLEASE!

*(Angela continues her story)*

Angela, I don't know how I could do what I did to him because I loved him so much.

*(She rips off another nail as Veronica continues to scream)*

Angela- But in the end I realized something, love…

*(Rips off another One)*

Angela- Love, love is just a word.

*(Rips off another one)*

*(We cut to black and come back to see that all of her nails had been removed with the pliers. Veronica is sitting there in pain and agony, crying, blood pouring down her fingers)*

Angela, now, all I want from you is your ears. No words, just listen.

*(Veronica is still moaning in pain)*

Angela- Luis will call Daniel, and he will tell him a story. A story that if you do not imprint in your brain, what happened here will be nothing compared to what will happen later. Now shut up! Luis llamarlo *(Call Him, Luis)*, *(Daniel starts dialing)*

Daniel- Luis?

Luis-Verónica tiene un problema, está bien, pero parece que los químicos que usaron en sus uñas causaron una reacción. la llevo al hospital ahora. *(Veronica has a problem, she's ok but it seems the chemicals they used on her nails caused a reaction. I am taking her to the hospital now)*

Daniel- Qué? Está ella bien, Estas segura *(What? Is she ok? Are you sure?)*

Luis- Ella está bien *(she's fine)*

Daniel- I'm coming now

Luis- stay..I will take her and bring her home shortly

Daniel- Ok, any news?

Luis- Nada concerniente.   *(nothing concerning)*

Daniel- Ok bene gracias Luis keep me informed.

*(Luis hangs up)*

Angela- Were you listening? *(Pulls up her head by her hair)*

Veronica- Ahhh! Si, yes, I understand, I understand. *(quivering as she answers)*

Angela- good, Luis will take you to the hospital. I suggest you shake this off quickly once you're all patched up.

Luis- Vamos. *(Let's go)*

## **INT Frankie's Laundry Mat**

*(The Don is in the back office on the phone, and in walks Angela)*

Don Gian- I'm... *(Pauses)* Gonna have to call you back *(hangs up)*. What an unpleasant surprise. I thought the arrangement was clear. You do your thing, and I do mine; you keep your house in order as I do mine.

Angela- Well... *(She walks around the chair before sitting)* that was the arrangement until something came up.

Don  Gian-What do you mean? What happened?

Angela- It seems my son's wife had a couple of interesting sexual encounters with your boy Joey, and I thought since no one got hurt, we should just talk instead of wagering a war.

Don Gian-OH? And your son... does he know?

Angela- What do you think?

Don Gian- What makes you think he won't find out?

Angela- Let's just say I've taken precautions.

Don Gian- And what kind of precautions do you intend me to take on Joey? I assume that is why you are here.

Angela-*(She leans over and whispers)* He needs to disappear…

*(She gets up and walks out while Don remains sitting in his chair, pondering the situation*

## **Int Joeys Apartment Rego Park Queens**

*(Joey is awakened by a phone call, still half asleep)*

Joey- Yah?!

Frankie- You up?

Joey- Yah, can't you hear it in my voice? *(Yawns)* I was just doing my morning cartwheels. It's 6:00 in the morning. What's up?

Frankie- Get your ass up and meet me by the café

Joey- Yah Yah, ok, ok *(yawns again)* ciao. *(bye)*

*(Hangs up)*

*(A short while later, Joey arrives at the café)*

Joey- What's up, Frankie Smalls? You couldn't find your dick, so you decided to get up early?

Frankie- Funny, No, my father wants to see us

Joey- He's here?

Frankie- In the back

*(They proceed to walk to the back of the office. Don is sitting there listening to music, a song called "Lu Me Sceccu," while Tony stands within his reach)*

Joey- Hey D…

*(Don cuts him off)*

Don Gian. Shh listen…

Joey- OK, but…

*(Don cuts him off again. He proceeds to tell them about the song that is playing)*

Don Gian- I love this song. It's about a donkey that is a very great breed, but he couldn't speak, and now he's dead and buried in the farmer's garden.

*(Frankie and Joey both look at each other, puzzled; Joey tries to get another word in)*

Joey- Don…

Don Gian- listen

*(The song finishes)*

Don Gian- It's such a beautiful song.

Joey- Yes, it's lovely. *(he shrugs his shoulder at Frankie like he doesn't know what's going on)*

Frankie- beautiful... *(sarcastically)*

*(Don just sits quietly, staring at Joey for a minute; Joey looks confused as to what is going on)*

Don Gian- So….you think I wouldn't find out huh?

*(He continues to stare at Joey)*

Don- You think you're capable of keeping secrets from me?

Joey- Don what do you mean? I don't have any secrets.

Don- So you're going to sit there and lie to me after everything I've done for you.

Joey- Don, I really don't know what you are referring to.

Don- You're right; maybe I am just mistaken. Maybe another Blond hair blue eyed Italian guy was seen fucking Daniels wife.

*(Joey becomes frozen as if he's staring into the oblivion)*

Don Gian- By the look on your face, I'm guessing I got it right the first time. Things are starting to come back to you. Huh? Your brain it's finally FUCKING WORKING!

*(Frankie, in shock and disbelief, puts his hands over his face)*

Don Gian- Now you listen and listen well. I want to see college applications filled out and mailed by the end of the week. No exceptions!

Joey- Don, please, I know I fucked up, but I did everything you asked of me. I finished high school and didn't get into any trouble. You promised me.

Don Gian- You're right, I did promise you. But you also promised me you would stay away from the Mexicans.

Joey- Please, Don, I appreciate everything… you accepting me into your home, getting me that apartment as a senior, everything. I'll be 18 tomorrow. I want to enter your family business. Please…

Don Gian- Basta! *(ENOUGH!) (Slams his hand on the table)* that's my final decision; now, get the fuck out of my office before I have you sleeping next to the donkey.

*(Joey begins to walk away very sad with his shoulders hunched over, he then turns back for a second)*

Joey- Does he know?

Don Gian-No, he doesn't, and it will stay that way. Do not contact her again, you hear me?!

*(Joey shakes his head yes as Tony puts a gentle hand on his shoulder and escorts him out. Frankie, following behind, is stopped by Don)*

Don Gian- Aspetta tu *(wait you)*. Weren't you supposed to keep an eye on him?

Frankie- I swear I didn't know.

Don Gian- Why do I have you here if that's your excuse? Let me be more specific with you. What does a baby do when the mother walks away?

Frankie- He follows her.

Don- Bingo! *(Takes two fingers and makes a gesture towards his eyes as if to say you better watch him more closely. Frankie stands a minute and then proceeds to catch up to Joey)*

Frankie- Joe, wait up *(jogs up to catch up to him);* what were you thinking?

Joey- I'm sorry, Frank. At first, it was a moment of weakness, but then I started to get to know her. I didn't mean for this to happen. I swear.

Frankie- You were playing a very dangerous game. You could have been killed or, worse, started a war if they found out. *(Sighs)* Listen, just go back to the apartment, relax a bit, and later, we will go to Mario's and have some drinks.

Joey- I'm really not in the mood for drinks tonight, Frank.

Frankie- Come on, let's go have a couple of drinks, and let's put this behind us. Hey, if you have to go away to college, you might as well have some fun before, no? Plus, you're 18 at midnight, soooo....

Joey- Ok. *(somberly)*

## **INT Daniela And Veronica House**

*(Luis and Veronica arrive home; sitting at the table is Daniel and his sister Maria)*

Daniel- Mi amor estas bien? qué pasó? *( my love are you ok)*

*(Veronica fingers all bandaged up with one partial fingertip showing)*

Luis- She…

*(Daniel cuts him off)*

Daniel- Cállate! *(Shut up)* I want to hear from her what happened.

Veronica- I went to Su's beauty parlor, as I told you yesterday, I don't know what they used or if it was an allergic reaction or something, but my fingers began to swell. When we got to the hospital, they had to remove my nails to stop the infection. They told me to take some pills for the pain; they said I would be fine and that the nails would take a few months to grow back.

Maria- I never heard of such a thing happening.

Daniel- and Luis, did you go back to Su's and find out what happened?

Luis- No, I figured it was just an allergic reaction.

Daniel- No, no, it wasn't. I think they are upset with all the business you have been stealing in the neighborhood, sis. *(turns to Maria)*

*(Daniel gets up in a hurry and walks out angrily while Maria yells towards him)*

Maria- Daniel, No!  Luis, go with him and make sure he doesn't kill anyone.

Luis- Si Maria.

*(Luis follows behind Daniel)*

Maria-Are you ok?

Veronica- Yes, I'll be fine. I just want to rest.

Maria- Yes, of course.

*(Maria gets up and starts walking toward the door; as she reaches her hand out to open she turns)*

Maria-Are you sure that's what happened?

Veronica- Yes, of course; why would I lie?

Maria-Ok *(walks out)*

# INT Maria's Beauty Salon

*(Angela walks in as Maria is sitting behind the front desk)*

Ángela- Hola hija. *(hello, daughter)*

María-Madre, ¿qué haces aquí? *(Mother, what are you doing here?)*

Ángela-Vamos a la parte de atrás y hablemos. *(Let's go to the back and talk)*

*(Miquel is in the office going over some receipts)*

Angela- Salir idiota. *(get out idiot)*

*(Miquel looks at Maria, and she nods as if to say, just go)*

Miquel- Si, no hay problema *(Yes, no problema)*

*(He exits)*

Maria-Why are you always treating my husband like shit?

Angela- Because he's an idiot.

Maria- He… is still your son-in-law.

Angela- I didn't come here to insult your husband. I came to talk to you about something.

Maria- Fine! But at least treat him with some respect; after all, he's helping me clean your dirty money.

Angela- You think people can't be replaced? Everyone can be replaced, even your husband.

Maria- Can you just tell me what you want? Everything is running smoothly here, so I don't know what it is you want from me.

Angela- It's not about the salon.

Maria- What then?

Angela- I'm going to need you to start doing a little more.

Maria- More? More than laundering your money?? You know, I wanted a legit business until you forced me into this.

Angela- If it wasn't for me, you wouldn't have a business. If you can't trust family, who can you trust right?

Maria- So, Mother, what else can I do for you *(sarcastically)*

Angela- I need you to start accompanying Jose on drops.

Maria- Daniel Does that.

Angela- Yah, well, I feel your brother is starting to unhinge.

Maria- Well, his wife just came home with no fingernails.

Angela- Yes, that was unfortunate.

Maria- You didn't have anything to do with that, did your mother?

Angela- Of course not! What kind of person do you think I am?

Maria- I know who I am talking to.

Angela- I just heard about it this morning. Why would I have anything to do with that? I like Veronica. It sounds like some sort of a freak accident.

Maria- Yah, "Freak accident"

Angela- So that's a yes, I presume?

Maria- If it gets you out of my shop, fine! And the salon?

Angela- Your stupid husband can oversee things while you're out.

Maria- So… my husband is an idiot? You don't like him, but you trust him to look after things?

Angela- Should I be worried?

Maria- No

Angela-Alright then!

*(Angela gets up and leaves, walking right past Miquel with some sort of evil smile)*

Miquel- What happened?

Maria-You will look after the salon when I'm out.

Miquel- She's ok with that?

Maria- It was her idea.

Miquel- She trusts me now?

*(Maria watches her mother walk into the car from the window)*

Maria-No, no, she doesn't. *(Looks back at Miquel)* Don't fuck up.

## **Int Joeys Apartment**

*(Joey, getting ready to leave his apartment, hears a knock on the door; it's Frankie)*

Frankie- Oh Wow!

Joey- What?

Frankie-Nothing, just if ugliness was a crime, you'd get the electric chair.

Joey- funny! Well, if laughter is the best medicine, your face must be curing the world.

Frankie, I don't know what makes you so stupid, but it really works for you.

Joey-I'm trying to see things from your point of view, but I can't get my head that far up my ass.

Frankie- He's back! *(Laughing)* Come on, let's go.

## **EXT Mario's Bar In Ridgewood Queens**

*(Frankie and Joey arrive by cab, walk up to the bouncer, and ignore the packed line to enter. The bouncer stops them)*

Bouncer- where are you going? Let me see your ID!

Joey- You want my ID? Here, here's my fucking ID. Look! "Forest hills High school 2010 graduating class".

Bouncer-I can't let you in, Bra…

Joey- Ok, take care and good luck, but by good luck, I mean go fuck yourself and by take care, I mean go fuck yourself.

*(They both stare at each other momentarily and begin laughing hysterically; Joey puts his ID in his back pocket).*

Bouncer- Happy birthday cuz I'm going to come in later and have a drink with you.

Joey- Sounds good, Jay.

Frankie- Joe, go get us a couple of drinks *(hands him money)*. I'll be there in a sec.

*(Joey goes in; Frankie stays a moment longer)*

Frankie- Jay, if you see any Mexicans you would recognize from the block, come in and let me know. Yes?

Jason- Anyone in particular?

Frankie- No, just anything that may seem suspicious to you.

Jason- You got it, Frank.

*(We cut inside; Joey spots Mario by the bar with the bartender)*

Joey- Hey yo, Mariooo.

Mario- Joey che Cazzo Fai!? *(Joey, what the fuck are you doing)*

Joey- I came to get wasted on my Birthday.

Mario- oh yah! *(Turns to the bartender)* Listen, you see this guy here. Anything he wants is on the house, you understand?

Bartender- You got it, Mario

Joey- Grazie Mario, I appreciate that.

Mario- The Don, he did so much for me; I owe him my life. He's a good man.

*(Joey takes a second to let that comment sink in)*

Joey- Oh Yah how?

Mario- You see this bar?

Joey- Yah?

Mario- He gave it to me.

Joey- He just gave it to you?

Mario- I was at a low point in my life, and he gave me a reason to live. He will always have a special place in my heart. Is Frankie here, too?

Joey- Yah, he's by the door talking to Jay.

Mario- OK, I'll come back and say hello; I gotta go set some stuff up. We'll talk more later.

Joey *(nods his head): Okay,* Mario.

*(Enter Frankie)*

Frankie-look who I found outside.

Joey- Sal Domani!

Sal- What's up cock smoker? What have you been up too?

Joey- Nothing much, just here having a drink with your mom. She's in the back giving someone a lap dance or maybe head… I don't know.

Sal- Same old joey. *(Laughs)*

Joey- Celebrating my 18th

Sal- Happy birthday, brother! What are you doing with life after high school?

Joey- Thinking of going to college is not my choice exactly, but it is what it is.

Sal- Nice! Good for you; I'll be working in my father's construction business. Listen, I have to go meet up with some people, but here's my card.  Let me know if anything changes. I can always use your handy hands on the site. Maybe ill come back, and we'll have a drink and catch up more later.

Joey- Ciao Sal

*(Sal leaves toward the back of the Bar)*

Frankie- shots?

Joey- shots...

Frankie- 2 shots of jaeger

*(The bartender brings the shots; Frankie and Joey each hold a shot in the air)*

Frankie –To our journey to bigger and better things, salute

Joey- Salute *(cheers)*

## **INT Viva Mexicana**

*(Angela's cell phone rings)*

Angela- si? Que? Este maldito Niño *(yes? what? this fucking kid)*, Ok

*(Hangs up)*

Angela- José, ve a buscar a Daniel para mí *(go get Daniel for me)*. Tell Luis to go watch over Veronica.

Jose-Si jefe,

## **INT Mario's Bar**

*(Joey is seen laughing and drinking heavily with Frankie and a few others, including Sal, Jay, the bouncer, and a few girls)*

Frankie- According <u>ONLY</u> to your age, you will legally be an adult soon.

Joey- According to your pants, I can legally call you Frankie smalls. *(Takes another shot and laughs)*

Girl - I don't see anything wrong with Frankie's pants.

Joey- That's because you're not looking hard enough.

*(Frankie laughs and begins to make a toast as the clock strikes midnight)*

Frankie-Joey, I love you like a brother; you are 18 today and legally able to do everything you have been doing since you were 15. I'm also sorry I hurt your feelings earlier when I called you stupid. I really thought you already knew. May the candles on your cake always outnumber your gray pubes! Buon compliano! *(happy birthday)*

Jay the bouncer- Happy birthday!

Sal- Salute! Happy birthday!

Joey- Frank, your father once told me that your birth certificate is an apology letter from the condom factory. Salute! *(Drinks another shot)*

Joey- How many mobsters does it take to throw a man down the stairs?

Girl- How many?

Joey- None. He fell *(drinks another shot)*

*(As they drink some more and joke, Joey overhears a conversation behind them)*

Person 1- I took my wife to Su's beauty salon earlier today, and you wouldn't believe what happened. This guy just storms in and pistol-whips the owner. He starts screaming over him. 'My wife Veronica was in the hospital all night.' What the fuck did you do to her!?

Person 2- Wow, did he shoot him?

Person 1 – No, a guy who was there grabbed him and dragged him out before the cops could get there.

*(Joey comes over and interrupts)*

Joey- I couldn't help but overhear; what did you say the girl's name was?

Person 1 – Veronica F  something I believe. Do you know her?

Joey- No, *(throws some money on the table)* next rounds on me.

*(Joey begins walking away toward the exit)*

Frankie- Where are you going, Joe?

Joey- I have to go drain the snake. Why do you want to hold it for me?

*(Frankie is watching Joey walk away and turns for a split second as joey exits the bar without his knowledge. Frankie then walks up to the two people)*

Frankie- Hey, that guy who was just here, what did he say?

Person 2- He was asking about a guy who beat up the owner of Su's beauty salon earlier today.

Frankie- What was his name?

Person 1- We don't know his name, but he was referring to his wife, Veronica.

*(Frankie is shocked and pissed off and rushes to the bathroom to look for joey; he's not there. He then goes to the bartender)*

Frankie- Hey, you seen Joey, blond hair, blue eyes? It was his birthday.

Bartender- Yah, he actually just left.

Frankie- fffuck!

Bartender- What happened?

*(Frankie ignores him and runs out of the bar in search of Joey)*

# INT Veronica And Daniel's House

*(Veronica is sitting alone at the table in the kitchen when she hears noise by the side living room window. She picks up a knife with her palm as her hands are all bandaged up)*

Veronica- Who's there? *(As she holds up the knife)*

Joey- It's ME V…

*(Joey falls in through the window, somewhat intoxicated)*

Veronica- Joey?? What the hell are you doing here?

Joey- *(slurring)* what happened to your hands??

Veronica- Are you drunk? You shouldn't be here.

Joey- Tell me what happened to your hands? Who did this?

Veronica- Daniel could be home any minute. Why are you here? You have to go.

Joey- I overheard two people mentioning how Daniel went to Su's salon and beat the owner half to death.

Veronica- What?

Joey- What the hell is wrong with him?

Veronica- He thinks they did this to my hands.

Joey- Well, if he didn't, then who did?

*(Veronica takes a long pause, wondering if she should tell him)*

Joey- V? Tell me

Veronica- I can't.

Joey- Why?

Veronica- I shouldn't.

Joey- Tell me, please!

Veronica- You have to promise me you won't say or do anything.

Joey- Ok, I promise. Now tell Me.?

Veronica- Angela knows about us.

Joey- What? She does? *(Begins getting nervous and looks around the room)*

Veronica- Yes, this was her doing. (lifts her hands) She told me to stay away from you or something far worse will happen.

Joey- Don knows too and told me the same thing, to stay away from you.

*(A car pulls into the driveway; its Luis)*

Veronica- you have to go, go, Joe!

*(Joey starts to climb back out the window)*

Veronica- Wait! *(Kisses joey)* happy birthday.

*(Veronica runs back toward the kitchen, and just as joey exits the window, his pants get caught, and they slowly start to fall. He struggles to lift his pants while crawling out of the side window. Without his knowledge, his ID had fallen out)*

# Chapter 3
# 'Pezzo' (Piece)

## <u>INT Angela Manson Bay Ridge, NY</u>

*(Angela is in her office inside her Manson in Bay ridge when Jose and Daniel Arrive)*

Jose- Jefe, the owner of the Chinese restaurant, is in a coma. Luckily, there were no video recordings, just a few witnesses. Do you want me to take care of that?

Angela- *(looks at Daniel)* Daniel, do you want Jose to take care of that?

Daniel- They hurt Veronica in revenge. Don't you remember what they did the day after she opened?

Angela- It is not up to you to decide what actions should be taken.

Daniel- She's my fucking wife!

Angela- Maybe your wife shouldn't have gone to get her nails done there; maybe your wife should have started to take responsibility for her actions. I am running a business! Are you trying to jeopardize that business?

Daniel- No, I a…

Angela- *(cuts him off)* and you still haven't answered my question. Do you or don't you want Jose to take care of it?

Daniel- Yes, mother.

Angela- great! Jose *(nods her head at Jose toward the door)*

*(Jose leaves, and Angela tries to focus her attention elsewhere)*

Angela- Maria will accompany Jose on pickups and drops from now on.

Daniel- Mother, no.

Angela- Are you going to stand there and question my decisions after all the shit you pulled?

Daniel-fine! *(Angrily)*

Angela-You will oversee Miquel and the salon. I need you to keep a close eye on your brother-in-law for me.

Daniel- Why?

*(Angela ignores him again)*

Daniel- Can you tell me if this is a permanent arrangement?

Angela- We will see.


## **INT Joeys' Apartment**

*(Its 11 am, and Joey wakes up and turns on the TV, "Breaking news two bodies have been recovered outside Mario's Bar and grill in Ridgewood Queens. The names of the victims are yet to be released" (but they show pictures of them instead)." In unrelated news, it seems the wife of one of the victims was also found dead in her apartment from strangulation. The police have no suspects at this time... We will return with more details shortly". Joey's memory is in flux, and he looks at the pictures more closely and is in shock when he realizes who they are...)*

Joey-fuck..

*(Hears a bang on the door, joey jumps off the couch)*

Joey- YAH! Who is it?

Frankie- Its Frankie, Open up.

*(Joey opens the door, and in walks Frankie and Tony)*

Joey- Its two early for a birthday party. My head is still pounding.

Frankie- Where did you run off to last night? You just disappeared.

Joey- It's still a little blurry, but the last thing I remember, I was going to the pisser and then woke up home to you two dumb fucks banging on my door. My head feels like it's been in a drum being banged on all night.

Tony- Get dressed, and let's go take a ride, ride. *(While eating a bagel)*

Joey- Where's my fucking bagel, huh T? It's my birthday!

Tony- Auguri, Auguri *(congrats, congrats. All distorted as he walks out eating his bagel)*

Joey- Jerkoff! *(Referring to Tony)*

Frankie- You don't remember anything, huh?

Joey- Geez, still Frank, no, I don't.

Frankie- When you went to the pisser, I asked the two guys about your conversation, Yah: about the incident at Su's with Daniela and Veronica.

Joey- Yah, so…? I overheard them and was interested in what happened.

Frankie- Then you disappeared, and the two guys you were talking too were found dead outside Mario's this morning. Tell me, Joe, what am I supposed to think?

Joey- You think I had something to do with that? Really?

Frankie- No, I don't, but I'm curious on where you went.

Joey- What do you want me to do if I can't remember? The Irish couldn't even keep up with me last night. *(He whispers to himself)*. I fucking hate leprechauns

Frankie- You think this is a game, Joe? What makes you think they won't come for you?

Joey- What's your problem? All of a sudden, your father gives you some responsibility, and you seem drunk with power?

Frankie- This has nothing to do with that. This has to do with you and how, if you continue this way, you will end up dead.

Joey- Why? Is your father asking you to off me now?

Frankie- No, Joe, the Mexicans are dangerous. If Daniel finds out, he will come for you.

Joey- Let that little Mexican come.

Frankie- Shit, Joe, just Get dressed.

Joey- Yes, boss! *(Sarcastically)*


# <u>INT Cafe Di Napoli.</u>

*(Don Gian's phone rings)*

Don Gian- Second time in two days, huh? Did you forget your knives in my back?

Angela- Oh shut up, Gian! I have another shipment coming in.

Don Gian- We just picked up a couple of days ago.

Angela- What can I say? It's Christmas, and I'm Santa Claus

Don Gian- That's a lot for even me to move.

Angela- I'll provide you with a little help.

Don Gian- That's not a good idea.

Angela- It will be fine. I assume you already told your son?

Don Gian- Was that not our agreement?

Angela- Yes, of course, Maria and Jose will stay for the drop and consult the distribution.

Don Gian- How long has she known?

Angela-It's been quite a while now. Is today good? Jose will be in contact with Tony.

Don Gian- VA bene. *(ok)*

Angela- I love it when you speak to me in Italian.

Don Gian- Oh Yah? Vaffanculo! *(Fuck you, and hangs up)*

*(Angela laughs)*

## __INT Tony's Car__

Joey- Where the hell we going?

Frankie- The library.

Joey- Seriously? The library? Are we teaching T to read? I knew you were a stuttering prick but didn't know you were an illiterate asshole too.

Frankie- You're going to apply to colleges online like you promised.

Joey- I don't need a chaperone, let alone two.

Frankie- Tony and I have to go handle something; there is no chaperone, just you. Why? Are you tired of hanging with me, brother?

Joey- I liked the old Frankie better. The one who didn't do everything T tells him to do.

Tony- You should take this out with your father, father.

Frankie- You already agreed to this, Joe.

Joey- I guess the apple doesn't fall far from the tree.

Frankie- What do you mean by that?

Joey- I used to like apples.

## **INT Café Di Napoli**

*(Charlie and Gino are at the café when Charlie receives a phone call; he walks outside to get some privacy)*

Charlie- Aloo

*(It's only a one-way conversation you don't hear the other end)*

Charlie- Secaucus, NJ

*(Conversation continues)*

Charlie- Ok

## **INT Car Outside The Library 5th Ave**

*(Frankie, Tony, and Joey arrive at the library)*

Frankie- Can I trust you to do what you need to do?

Joe-Can I trust you not to be a slithering asshole?

Frankie- love you too.

*(Joey gets out and slams the door behind him. They wait to see that he enters the building, and knowing that they are watching, he proceed into the library; once the car takes off, Joey comes back outside and makes a call)*

Joey- Sal!

Sal- What's up, kid?

Joey- Can you pick me up in the city?

Sal- Yah, sure, I'll tell the boys to finish up the job. Give me like 30.

## **INT Astoria Warehouse**

*(Tony and Frankie arrive at the warehouse, and to Frankie's surprise, he sees Maria and Jose. He whispers to Tony)*

Frankie- I thought this was only a drop for them. Why are they here?

Tony- Things have changed, changed.

Jose- Tony

Tony- Jose, Jose

Jose- this is Maria, Angela's daughter.

Tony- pleasure, pleasure, this is Frankie, Don Gian's son, son.

Maria- Hi

Frankie- Hello

*(Frankie is mesmerized by her beauty while Maria doesn't even give him a second look.)*

Tony- You won't be delivering cargo to our distributors correct, correct?

Jose- No, we are merely here to land a hand on trucks, as we know you are short on. We will use Viva Mexicana trucks.

Frankie- Then why are we here? You could have simply left the keys and the trucks.

Jose-That's a good point however, Angela and Gian…

*(Frankie cuts him off, feeling annoyed by the error as if it was intentional)*

Frankie- Its Don Gian.

Jose- Yes, of course. Don Gian and Angela agreed it would be best if the partnership continued with a more face-to-face arrangement.

Frankie- Why is that?

Jose- You and Maria will now be solely in charge of the pickup and distribution. Tony and I will be overseeing other aspects of our business arrangements.  The drops will come more frequently and often than a month's time.

*(Maria seems annoyed at the fact that she will have to deal with Frankie; Frankie seems to relish this change)*

Frankie-*(turns to Tony)* I can handle it.

Maria- OK then, if my job is done here.

*(Maria just walks out)*

Jose- she will warm up to you. We have about 200 kilos. Please get the product out of here as soon as possible. Tony, I will be in touch. Frankie, it was nice to meet you.

Frankie- Yah.

Tony-Jose, Jose.

*(Jose leaves as Tony and Frankie have a conversation)*

Tony- Call some of the boys and tell them they will have to make another trip, trip. For now, move it to NJ. Take my keys; I have something to handle in Cali. So I will take a load to Stelleti.  Take this, this *(hands Frankie a gun)*

Frankie- No problem T *(As he stares at his Glock)*

*(Tony loads a truck and proceeds to head to California; Not to his knowledge, a car is following him)*

## EXT Library

*(Joey is seen texting)*

Joey- I need to see you today.

*(Veronica's texting is in disarray due to her hands)*

Veronica- Otay, Danial gos to the saln I'l try an shakLuis.

Joey- Where I met you?  5 o'clock?

Veronica- OOL

*(Sal pulls up in his truck)*

Sal- joey boombatz.

Joey- Sal, pensa a domani. *(Sal, think of tomorrow)*

Sal- Get in!

Joey- Thanks, cuz.

Sal- After all you did for me in high school, anything for you. Where we going?

Joey- Queens...

## **INT - Maria' Beauty Salon**

Miquel- Daniel, come esta? *(how are you)*

Daniel- Buen Miquel, I've come to help you with the salon.

Miquel-Maria no me dijo nada. *(Maria didn't tell me anything)*

Daniel- Mi Madre me dijo que nos guste o no, estamos juntos. *(My mother told me whether we like it or not, we are together)*

*(Miquel seems shocked)*

## **EXT Forest Park**

Joey- leave me here. I'll be back in a min.

Sal- ok

*(Joey proceeds to walk in the park to the miracle round but he sees no one there. Texts veronica)*

Joey- I'm here; where are you?

*(Joey waits about 15 minutes with no answer, he begins to get worried. As he is about to leave, he receives a message from Veronica's phone, but it's Luis)*

Luis- Weren't your instructions clear?

*(Joey, angry and pissed off, walks to Sal's car)*

Sal- What's up?

Joey- I'm done taking shit from people!

Sal- Here… take this *(Hands Joey a Gun)*

*(Joey looks at it for a moment, and they peel off)*

# Chapter 4

# Rat

<u>**INT Café Di Napoli**</u>

Don Gian- Gino, dov'è Charlie? *(Where's Charlie?)*

Gino-ha chiamato prima. ha detto che sua momma è malata *(he called earlier. he said his mother is sick)*

Don Gian- Ancora il problema al cuore. *(Still the problem with her heart)*

Gino- Si. *(yes)*

Don Gian- starai bene da solo qui? *(you will be ok by yourself here?)*

Gino- sì, starò bene *(yes I'll be fine)*

*(Don Picks up his cell)*

Don Gian- Frankie, where are you?

Frankie- I'm on my way back from jersey.

Don Gian- Joey?

Frankie- I believe he is still at the library where we dropped him off.

Don Gian- OK, make sure. His phone has been off all day. Voglio dire buon compleanno prima che finisca la giornata. *(I want to say happy birthday before the day is up)*

Frankie- Ok.

# <u>INT Tony's Car Somewhere In PA</u>

*(Tony, already in PA, looks in the rear view mirror and notices a car has been following him. He decides to stop at a deli. He proceeds to go in. That same car pulls up across the street and waits. A big truck blocks the view inside. Just as this unknown person tries to move around to locate Tony inside the store, a gun is pointed at his head; it's Tony)*

Tony- Unlock the door and keep your hands up.

Charlie- T, It's me, Charlie.

Tony- shut up up!

*(Tony gets in the car and directs Charlie to drive; they pull up to an abandoned building)*

Tony- Get out, out! *(Pointing gun at him)*

Charlie- Tony, Don told me to follow you and make sure everything was ok.

*(Tony shoots him in the Knee, Charlie screams in anguish)*

Charlie- AHHHHHH!

Tony- riprova, riprova. *(try again)*

Charlie- I'm telling you the truth.

*(Tony shoots him in the other knee)*

Tony- Lie to me again; the next one is in your head, head.

Charlie- Ok, ok, don't shoot! Era Bimino

*(Tony shoots him in the head)*

Tony- Hai scelto la parte sbagliata, sbagliata. *(You chose the wrong side)*

*(Tony takes all his belongings, burns the vehicle with Charlie's body inside and leaves)*

## <u>EXT Outside Veronica And Daniel's House</u>

*(Joey and Sal are sitting inside the car parked half way down the block)*

Sal- What are we doing here?

Joey- Checking on someone.

*(Luis and Daniel pull up and start walking toward the house; Joey opens the door with a gun in hand. As he steps out, he gets pulled back in.)*

Sal- Wait!

Joey- What?

Sal- Cops.

Joey- Shit!

*(Joey gets back in the truck as soon as he looks over, Frankie pulls up beside them)*

Frankie- Of course, where else would you be right?

Joey- What the fuck are you doing here, Frank?

Frankie- The question is, what the fuck you doing here Joe?

Sal- Frank.*(nods at Frankie)*

Frankie- Get in, Joe!

Joey- No thanks.

Frankie- I'm trying to protect you.

Joey- You are trying to protect yourself. I'm not part of that family.

Frankie- My family is your family.

Joey- No, you made that perfectly clear.

Frankie- Why do you think that?

Joey- When were you going to tell me Daniel's mother knew all along?

Frankie- Knew what all along?

Joey- Don't play stupid with me, Smalls, Veronica told me.

Frankie- I didn't know, I swear!

Joey-. Veronica told me everything. I think your father's the rat! It's a cold business, right Frank.

*(Joey shows Frankie the gun)*

Frankie- Please, Joe, don't do anything stupid.

Joey- I'm done taking orders from you, your father, and Tony twice the dick DiMaggio. Fuck off!

*(The truck peels off; Frankie does not follow in pursuit)*

## __INT Angela House__

*(Phone rings)*

Ángela- Si?

Jesús Mendoza- hola Ángela. *(hello Ángela)*

Ángela- Jefe, cómo está? *(boss how are you?)*

Jesús- Me sentiré mejor una vez que garantices puedes mover todo el producto  duplicado. *(I will feel better once you guarantee me that you can move all the doubled product)*

Ángela- Todo ya está en movimiento. *(Everything is already in motion)*

Jesus- bueno, odiaría que algo saliera mal especialmente para usted. *(good, I would hate for something to go wrong, especially for you)*

Angela- Entiendo, Todo va bien. *(I I understand, everything is moving smoothly)*

Jesus- Mind if we speak in English? I need to better learn the language. *(accent)*

Angela- Yes, of course.

Jesus- I heard you are no longer using Joaquin twins on the West Coast. Is there some kind of problem? I would hope not...

Angela- I have my own contacts for the West Coast, and the product is selling more than it used to with the Joaquin twins.

Jesus- Very well, but remember you can always be accountable for your actions.

Angela- Yes, of course.

Jesus- Siempre es un placer hablar con usted *(always a pleasure to speak with you)*. We will talk soon, ciao.

Angela- Contigo también. *(With you as well)*

*(Phone hangs up)*

Angela-Maricón! *(Pussy)*

# <u>INT Barone Household In Middle Village Queens</u>

*(Phone rings)*

Don Gian- Tony, dove sei arrivato? *(Where did you arrive?)*

Tony-Ohio, Ohio

Don Gian- Tutto bene? *(All good)*

Tony- No avevo una macchina sulla coda, era Charlie, Charlie *(I had a car on my tail, it was Charlie)*

Don Gian- Charlie? Gino mi disse che sua momma era malata, bastardo! *(Gino told me his mother was sick, bastard)*

Tony- Bimino, bimino..

Don Gian- Bimino? quel serpente! *(That snake)*

Tony-tutto è stato gestito, gestito *(Everything has been managed)*

Don Gian- Significa che bimino è vicino, più vicino di quanto pensassimo. *(That means bimino is close, closer than we thought)*

Tony- Vado a Chicago, Chicago? sono vicino, vicino. *( I go to Chicago?, i am close, close)*

Don Gian- Si, come abbiamo discusso, devo andare, scopa mi sta chiamando sull'altra linea *(Yes, how we discussed, I have to go, Scopa is calling on the other line)*

Don Gian- Marco! Com'e  bello napoli? *( How is beautiful Napoli?)*

Marco Scopa-Sempre bella*(always beautiful)*, ascolta, ho sentito tante volte da Armando che non è incluso nella riunione delle 5 famiglie, Perché ?

*(Listen, I have heard several times from Armando that he is no longer included in the meeting of the 5 families. Why is that?)*

Don Gian-con tutto il rispetto Marco non posso fidarmi di lui *(With all due respect Marco i cannot trust him)*

Marco-Si tratta ancora di Josephine? *(Is this still about Josephine?)*

Don Gian-Sì, pensa ancora che avevo ucciso sua sorella *(yes he still thinks i killed his sister)*.

Marco- Ma questo è andato avanti abbastanza lungo. Fare la pace o le cose dovranno cambiare. non possiamo avere sangue cattivo *(This has gone on long enough. make peace or things will need to change. We cannot have bad blood)*

Don Gian- Ho capito capo *( I understand, boss)*

Marco- Bene! Ci sentiamo presto Ciao *(talk to you soon good! bye)*

Don Gian- Ciao.

*(Phone disconnects)*

Don- Figlio di puttana! *(Son of a bitch)*

## **INT Sal's Apartment In Fresh Meadows**

Joey- I appreciate you letting me crash here tonight.

Sal- If you need anything, let me know.

Joey- Hey, do you remember that time we convinced the deli clerk to pay us for protection?

Sal- YAH! *(Laughs)* We were the ones fucking up his store. We were protecting him from us.

*(Laughing)*

Joey- We did some fun shit in high school

Sal- If you don't go to college, we can always partner back up. I mean, my father's construction business is no legit business either. Things tend to fall into grey areas, just like your father's business.

Joey- That might be a distinct possibility, given the way they have been treating me.  They think I'm a child, and they need to make decisions for me, fuck them! I need to get rid of this phone.

Sal-I got you, here! *(Throws Joey a burner phone)*

*(Before Joey disconnects his phone, he receives a text)*

Veronica- It's me. I need to see you. Tomorrow night, Juniper Park, 10 pm?

*(Joey remains staring at the message for a moment)*

Sal- What's up?

Joey- Veronica.

Sal- The girl you were supposed to meet at the park?

Joey- Yah.

Sal- Trap?

Joey- I don't know.

## **Int Barone Home**

Frankie- I caught up to Joey outside veronica house with sal

Don Gian- E dove sta? *(And where is he)*

Frankie- They sped off.

Don – Quando ascoltera questo Ragazzo? *(When will this kid listen),* let him be for tonight; look for him in the morning. I have bigger things to think about right now.

*(Frankie keeps to himself. Joey having a gun to not overwhelm his father with bad news)*

Frankie- Why? What's going on?

Don Gian – We need to make peace with Bimino.

Frankie- Fuck Him! He's still blaming you for her? She made her own choice and he needs to accept the fact that she left all of us, not just him!

Don Gian- It's not that simple. You can't go against Scopa; they will reorganize.

Frankie- Are they still in the dark about the Mexicans?

Don Gian- I'm not sure; Charlie was the Bimino rat.

Frankie- Charlie? Really..

## **INT Veronica And Daniels House**

*(Daniel and Luis are speaking inside one of the rooms in the house when Luis leaves and Daniel joins Veronica in the living room)*

Daniel- Do you know how bad I want to smack you right now? Because of you, I have to play babysitter to Maria's husband instead of doing what I need to do.

Veronica- You didn't have to do what you did.

Daniel- I go there and defend your honor as my wife, and this is how you repay me?

*(He lifts his hands up as if to smack her)*

Veronica- Such a model husband you are…

*(Daniel picks up a lamp and throws it over her head, and it shatters everywhere. He then pulls out his gun and presses it against her head)*

Daniel- Do you like my modal hand gun!?

Veronica- You won't…

*(Daniel grabs her face and stares at her for a minute)*

Daniel- I won't?

*(He presses the gun harder to her head and hesitates a minute before pushing her head away)*

Daniel- Go upstairs! Get the fuck out of my face. Rata callejera. *(Street Rat)*

*(Veronica goes upstairs as Daniel begins to pick up the pieces of the lamp; just then, a glare catches his eye. He reaches under a chair, thinking it is glass, but to his surprise, he finds Joey's ID)*

Daniel- Hijo de puta! *(Son of a bitch)*

# Chapter 5

# Till Death Do Us Part

## <u>EXT Veronica And Daniel House</u>

*(Luis is banging on the door and looking through the window; all of a sudden, we see Frankie pull up in his car. Luis notices and points in his direction)*

Luis- Frankie?

Frankie- Who wants to know?

Luis- It's Luis. I work with Jose. What are you doing here?

*(Frankie plays it off as car trouble)*

Frankie- My car was idling high, so I pulled over.

Luis- You don't say? Hey, you have a brother, right? Joey or something like that?

Frankie- why do you ask?

Luis- No reason, just curious. Relax….we are business associates.

*(Frankie starts to get worried about Joey's safety but feels the need to counter back aggressively)*

Frankie- Oh wow, I didn't even notice. Doesn't Daniel Live here?

*(Luis, taking offense/threatened, walks up to Frankie's car window, stares at him for a moment, and then begins to reach out. Frankie, believing he has a gun, has his hand on the gun placed beside the left side of the chair)*

Luis- Nice to meet you *(sticks out his empty hand for a shake)*

*(Frankie hesitates but decides to extend his hand to shake. Luis, with a tight grip, holds on to his hand a bit longer as Frankie yanks it back)*

Luis- I'll see you around, Frankie

*(Frankie watches Luis leave from the mirrors of his car as he sits a moment longer, visibly shaken)*

## **<u>INT Maria's Beauty Salon</u>**

Luis- Miquel.

Miquel- Luis come esta? *(How are you Luis?)*

Luis- donde esta Daniel? *(Where is Daniel?)*

Miquel- He was here yesterday, but I haven't seen him today.

Luis- E Verónica? You see her?

Miquel- No I haven't.

*(Maria walks in)*

Maria- Que paso Luis? *(What happened, Luis?)*

Luis- Nada, you see your brother or Veronica today?

Maria- I called Daniel yesterday, but he didn't pick up. Is everything ok?

Luis- Si, I just need to speak with him. If you hear from him, let me know.

Maria- I will.

# INT Tony's Car

*(Tony, Passing Chicago on Route 66, picks up his phone to make a call)*

Johnny Stelleti- Tony

Tony- Johnny, I'll be there tomorrow night Night.

Johnny- I thought you would be here by morning.

Tony- I need to make a detour again.

Johnny- Where?

Tony- I'll see you tomorrow, tomorrow.

Johnny- Ok, I need that shipment as early as possible.

Tony- ciao, ciao.

*(Hangs up)*

*(Tony quickly merges off the highway and exits. The Sign reads Chicago 10 miles.*

# INT Café Di Napoli

Frankie- Gino... Did you see Joey around today?

Gino- For the first fucking time, I haven't seen that braciola all day.

Frankie- Stop eating the fucking cannoli's Gino. They are for customers.

Gino- what? I'm hungry. I didn't have breakfast.

Frankie- fucking elephant. If you hear from him, tell him to call me ASAP.

*(Gino face is stuffed with cannoli)*

Gino-*(distorted)* OAKAY

# <u>EXT Sanitation Lot In Chicago</u>

*(Tony pulls up to a sanitation lot from a block away with binoculars in hand. He notices Angelo and Armando Bimino having a discussion. Tony sits for a minute and watches, then pulls away. We then cut to a house in Lincoln Park, Chicago. Tony slips to the back of the house, where he disconnects the security alarm and slips through the window. He walks upstairs to a back office, where he snoops around and gathers together some papers. He folds them, puts them in his back pants, covers them with a shirt, and then proceeds to leave. All of a sudden, a woman walks in, and Tony hides. The woman comes upstairs, and Tony ducks behind the desk. The woman comes into the office; Tony has a gun in hand, thinking he will have to kill her, but miraculously, the woman forgets something and proceeds to walk out. Tony, noticing this, sneaks to the stairs and makes his way out of the house, where he runs into a neighbor)*

Neighbor- Hello, are you a friend of the family?

Tony- Do you have to a minute to talk about Jesus Christ, our lord and savior savior?

*(The neighbor is shocked)*

Neighbor- Um, I forgot my stove on, excuse me.

*(We cut to the sign on the neighbor's door reads no trespassing, especially if you are a Jehovah's witnesses)*

# <u>EXT Juniper Valley Park In Middle Village Queens</u>

*(Joey is at Juniper Park awaiting Veronica's arrival. A car pulls up; a person in a hoodie comes out of the car. Joey is confused about whether it is veronica or not, as the street lighting is missing. The Person pulls down his hoodie, and it's Daniel)*

Daniel- You thought you could just fuck my wife, puto!?

*(He walks by his trunk)*

Daniel- Say Hello Puta!

*(Veronica screaming for help from the trunk)*

Veronica- HELP PLEASE!

*(Daniel continues walking away from the car and toward Joey. He turns and pulls out his gun, and fires)*

Joey- NOOO!

*(Daniel then pulls his gun back around toward Joey, and a shot is fired…Its Sal from under the bleachers. He strikes him in the thigh. Joey then pulls his gun from his waist as Daniel tries to bring his arm around to aim at joey, and another shot is fired straight through Daniel's heart. Joey freezes for a moment, realizing what he has just done, and then runs toward the trunk of the car. He opens it… Veronica lays dead after a shot through the head)*

# <u>INT Bimino Household Chicago IL</u>

Armando bimino- figlio hai scoperto qualcosa? *(Son did you find out anything)*

Angelo Bimino- Incontrano in un magazzino nel New Jersey. *(They meet in a warehouse in NJ.)*

Armando- Cosa stai combinando gian? *(What are you up too Gian?)*

Angelo- Sei ancora convinto che fosse lui? *(Your still convinced it was him?)*

Armando- I don't have the proof, but I'm sure of it.

Angelo- It's been years, and we have no proof that Zio Gian killed Aunt Josephine.

Armando- Do not call him Zio! He doesn't deserve that respect! He doesn't want me in these meetings for a reason. Sta nascondendo qualcosa *(he's hiding something )*

Angelo- He doesn't want you in the meetings because you keep blaming him for her death.

Armando-  **Whose side are you on?** è responsabile lo so ! *(He's responsible; I know it!)*

Angelo- Yours, of course, but the police had ruled it a suicide. She was his wife. How can you still believe that?

Armando- My sister had no reason to kill herself, and if she did, he drove her to do it, which means HE IS RESPONSIBLE! Before you forgive him, remember how we have been treated the last few years like garbage! Get some of the boys together. We were going to pay my cognate *(brother in law)* a visit.

# Chapter 6
# Conseguenze (Consequences)

## <u>INT- Maria's House</u>

*(Maria sits on the couch emotional and upset)*

Maria- I can't believe it!

Miquel- Do you know who might have done this?

*(Maria takes a long pause as she sits there with tears in her eyes and an upset demeanor)*

Miquel- You know, don't you?

Maria- Stop it! I don't.

Miquel- Dime? *(Tell me?)*

*(Maria breaks down and tells Miquel everything)*

Maria- We have been working with the Italians for a while now. Daniel had no idea, and it may have gotten him killed.

*(Miquel shocked)*

Miquel-what? Are you serious, who did it? Is Jesus aware?

Maria- I don't know who, but Jesus does not know, and we need to keep it that way.

Miquel- I have something to confess as well.

Maria- Miquel? What?

Miquel- Please do not get mad at me, but I have been skimming money from the salon for a year now.

Maria- Miquel! No! Why?

Miquel- I wanted to set something apart. If something happens, we can leave and never look back.

Maria- My mother's going to kill you. Why would you do that?

Miquel- We needed a way out, and I think we should take it now and go.

Maria-Miquel, not only did you put yourself in danger with my mother, but if Jesus finds out, you may as well shoot me, too.

Miquel- They won't find out; I used to be a really good accountant, if you recall.

Maria- you just put us both on death row. How could you do that without telling me?

*(The door opens, and Luis and Jose walk in. Maria and Miquel suddenly stop talking)*

Jose- Both of you will need to stay with your mother for the time being.

Maria- What are you going to do about this? My brother is dead!

Jose- It will be taken care of; Luis will take you to your mother's now.

Maria- Jose, promise me you will kill whoever's responsible!

*(Jose looks at Maria for a moment before he exits)*

## **INT Angela House**

*(Police are at the residence questioning Angela on the death of her son)*

Detective Morrow- do you know anyone who would want to hurt your son?

*(Angela- staring straight with a blank/angry stare)*

Detective Morrow- Ma'am, I know this is a difficult time, but anything you can tell me to help find the person who killed your son? We have some reason to believe this could be a retaliation of an assault in Ridgewood. I have some eye witnesses stating Daniel was at the scene of the assault.

Angela- I don't know anything about that.

Detective- Anything you can remember to get us going on this investigation would be helpful. Anything at all.

Angela- I just told you I don't know! Don't you think if I knew something, I would tell you? That is my son who was shot dead!

Detective Morrow- I know this is a difficult time, but here is my card. If anything comes up, please give me a call.

*(The detective is reaching out to give Angela the card, but she ignores him, staring in the distance)*

Detective morrow- I will leave it here on your coffee table. I'm sorry for your loss.

## **EXT Forest Hills Lake**

*(Joey stands a moment, staring at the lake. Sal, by his side, does not say a word. Joey proceeds to throw two guns and two cell phones into the river)*

Sal- we have to go. We can't be seen here.

*(Joey takes another pause and proceeds to leave with Sal, not saying a word. They get in the car, and Joey askes to borrow his phone. Sal hands it to him. He proceeds to make a call)*

Joey- I'll meet you at the house.

## EXT Stelleti Warehouse CA

*(Tony is seen driving into a warehouse, where he is then greeted by Johnny stelleti)*

Johnny- Tony, come stai?

Tony- volevo che tu fossi l'unico a saperlo. bimino sta andando giù, giu *(i wanted you to be the only one to know. Bimino has to go down ,down)*

Johnny-che è successo *(what happened)*

Tony-They turned Charlie into a rat. suggerisco di guardare la tua famiglia un po 'più vicino, vicino. *(I suggest looking at your family a little closer)*

Johnny- cosa? Veramente? *(What? Really?)*

Tony- Si, Si. portami all'aeroporto. abbiamo anche altre questioni urgenti per quanto riguarda il nostro fornitore, fornitore*(take me to the airport. we also have other pressing matters regarding our supplier)*

Johnny- Minchia O.. Sempre I problemi *(damn, always problems)*

## INT Don Gian House

*(Sal drops off Joey in front of the Don's house)*

Sal- If you need me, brother, just let me know.

Joey- Thanks, Sal…for everything.

*(Sal nods and then drives off. You see two men behind the gate with guns. They proceed to let Joey in, and we see Frankie standing by the entrance)*

Frankie- You ok, Joe?

Joey- Yah, I'm fine.

*(Don Gian enters and walks up to Joey. He back-slaps him hard across the face with his right hand. Joey's demeanor is down, and he just takes the hit with no retaliation; he then grabs him and hugs him tight. Joey is taken by surprise but embraces the hug. The Don then pulls away to grab Frankie toward him as well)*

Don Gian- They will come. We have to be ready.

*(Don reaches into his back and hands Joey a gun)*

Don Gian- You get rid of the other one?

Joey- In the lake with the phones.

Don Gian- You taught yourself well. Stick together. You understand me, No matter what!

Frankie- Yes

Joey- We will, and Tony?

Don Gian- Tony is handling a few things out west, but he will be back tonight. Gino's going to pick him up. Frankie, I need you to call some of the boys in Brooklyn. We all stay here tonight.

*(Don Gian leaves the room to his office and makes a call)*

Don Gian- Can we talk about this? He was defending himself.

Angela- You didn't want them to know, so now you will pay for it…

*(Dial tone)*

# Chapter 7
# Revenge

## INT JFK Airport

*(We see Gino waiting in arrivals for Tony when he suddenly spots him)*

Gino- T over here

Tony- Things good, good?

Gino- Yah, everyone is by the dons.

## EXT Dons House

*(It's all quiet outside. After a few minutes you begin to see mob employees being shot one by one with a silencer.  One of them takes a flowerpot with him as he falls, it make a loud sound)*

Don Gian- They're here... go.

*(Don Gian orders two men upstairs. Frankie and Joey take refuge behind the couch while the don waits behind the door. One of the men upstairs is shot and falls out the window. The other man is able to take out the person with the silencer crouched behind the pushes. Just then 2 more men come up to the porch and kill the second man at the upstairs window. Don Gian looks through the peephole and shots one cartel member through the door. Another man kicks the door open, it hits Don in the eye and the force tosses him to the floor. The cartel member walks up to Don ready to shot but is shot in the head by Joey from behind the couch. Another races through the door and Frankie shoots him in the arm and disarms him. Don begins punching him and beating him to*

*death when we see someone in the window behind Frankie as they take aim… Bang! Tony shots him from behind. He comes into view of the window and shouts)*

Tony- We have to go, go

*(Frankie and joey help up Don and proceeds to scatter toward the car, where Gino is awaiting. Then, all of a sudden you hear another gun shot and Frankie Drops to the floor. Joey turns around as fast as he can and begins firing 1,2,3,4,5,6 shots until empty and continues to pull the trigger, click click click, whilst he screams in anger. Frankie is seen bleeding and in pain)*

Don Gian- you're going to be ok my boy, it's going to be ok. sii forte.*(your strong)*

*(They all lift him up and place him in the car as Tony goes back and pours something over the blood left by Frankie. Joey is holding his wound in the car to slow the bleeding)*

Don Gian- A casa di Vincenzo, Vai presto! *(Vincenzo's house hurry!)*

*(Another cartel member shoots at the car as they drive off. Midway through drive Don Asks Gino to drop him)*

Don Gian- Leave me here Gino. I will meet you at Vincenzo's. Frankie, stay strong. Joey take care of him.

Frankie- where you going? (whilst in agony)

Joey- I promise I will.

Don Gian- I'll be there real soon I promise. Stay strong my son.

# INT Angela House

*(Angela sitting in her chair in her office awaiting a call)*

Angela- Is it done?

Don Gian- OH! We are done alright!

Angela- Gian! Did you get my message?

Don Gian- My son is dead! *(angrily)*

Angela- good, That makes us even!

*(Don hangs up)*

# INT Vincenzo House Family Doctor

Joey- Is my brother going to be ok?

Vincenzo- He was shot one inch from his heart, he's lucky to be alive.

*(Joey, Gino and Tony are relieved to hear the news)*

Vincenzo- He just needs to rest.

*(In walks Don)*

Don Gian- How is he doc?

Vincenzo- He will make it Don.

Don Gian- Grandi notizie! Grazie vincenzo *(great news, thank you Vincenzo)*

Vincenzo- Prego, Don. *(Your welcome Don)*

*(Don pulls Tony to the side)*

Don Gian- She thinks Frankie's gone we bought ourselves a little time.

# EXT Parking Lot Frankie's Wash

*(The Don and Tony waiting in the parking lot in the back of Frankie's wash. A police car approaches)*

Officer Matteo- You're a hard man to find. Good thing Tony's name is on the wash.

Don Gian- Lets keep it that way. You have the papers?

Officer Matteo- Yah right here and ready to go.

*(Tony hands him an envelope in return)*

Officer Matteo- Listen Don, there are a lot of cops looking for you. Even I can't help. Your house was littered with bodies. It has become FBI jurisdiction; I hope you know someone in the FBI because this won't go away so easy.

*(Don turns to Tony)*

Don Gian- Do we know anyone in the FBI?

Tony-Lorenzo, Lorenzo.

Don Gian- AHH lorenzo, si..

Officer Matteo- I would be careful there is an FBI detective on the case; Detective Morrow and he's as straight as they come.

# INT Frankie's Wash

*(The Don and Tony are discussing their next move in his office when 3 individuals are escorted in by a Mob employee)*

Mob employee (Nicola) - Pulito *(clean, relating to weapons)*

Armando Bimino- cognate *(Brother in law)*

*(Don Gian not really shocked as he had a feeling Bimino would show up sometime soon)*


Don Gian-Armando, Angelo. che spiacevole sorpresa. *(What an unpleasant surprise)*

Armando- è passato molto tempo. *(A lot of time has passed)*

Don Gian- non mi dispiace che tu stia visitando, ma se si tratta ancora di Josephine puoi tornare sull'aereo a Chicago. *(I don't mind you visiting but if this is still about Josephine you can jump right back on the plane to Chicago)*

Armando- what kind of greeting is that? I just want to know the whole story. You owe me that.

Don Gian- I told you everything. I came home from the Bakery and I found her in the bathtub from a gunshot wound to the head. What more do you want me to say?

Armando- I don't believe you. There is more to this story.

Don Gian- She was my wife! Why would I do anything to hurt her?

Armando- That's what I'm trying to figure out.

Don Gian- This is what you came all the way to NY for?

Armando- well, you never pick up my call, so..

Don Gian- Cazzo pero! That's because you keep accusing me of having something to do with her death.

Angelo-Calma. *(calm down)*

Don Gian- Nipote, pensi che abbia avuto a che fare con la morte di tua zia? *(Nephew, you think I had something to do with your Aunt's death?)*

Angelo-That's not my call to make.

Don Gian- I got an idea; how about you convince yourselves to get the fuck out of my office.

Armando- Non è finite *(it's not over)*

Don Gian- Vafancolo! *(Go fuck yourself)* Nico! Escort them out please.

*(Nicola escorts them out as they seem agitated)*

Don Gian- **Porca miseria!** *(Son of a bitch)*

## **INT Vincenzo House**

*(Frankie wakes up from being medicated)*

Joey- Frank, how you feeling?

Frankie- Medium Well I guess.

Joey- *(laughs)* what are you a fucking steak? You sure you weren't shot in the head?

Frankie- if I was shot in the head id be repeating myself like Tony.

Joey- Is that what happened?

Frankie- Apparently, he told me a couple weeks back.

Joey- Shit! Now I feel bad for fucking with him this whole time.

Frankie-its ok, you didn't know.

Joey- I'm so glad you're ok. I'm sorry frank.

Frankie- We'll always be brothers. Listen Joe there is something you need to know.

*(We cut back after the conversation ends)*

Joey- I need some air.

Frankie- Stay calm, Joe.

Joey- I'm just going right outside I need a minute.

Frankie- ok.

*(Once outside, Joey begins walking away from the House)*

## **EXT Warehouse Secaucus NJ**

Angelo- This is the address.

Armando- Angelo, go around back. Anthony, Marco, come with me.

*(Armando looks through the window and the warehouse seems empty just for a pallet in the middle of the room. They break in and walk up to the pallet and open it. To their surprise it is filled a quarter of the way with cocaine. A couple seconds pass and you hear Freeze!)*

Cops- Let me see your hands. Get down with your hands behind your back!

*(The place is surrounded by police officers. Angelo sees what is happening and escapes through the back fence. He is not seen leaving)*

Officer Matteo- That's a lot of cocaine you got here.10 kilos?

Second officer- Looks more like, 10-12 to me.

Armando- It's not mine! I was set up!

<u>Officer</u> Matteo- We will see about that.

# Chapter 8
# La Verità (The Truth)

<u>**INT 104 Precinct**</u>

Armando- I'm telling you, that was not mine.

Officer Matteo- Interesting; considering these papers indicate that you purchased this warehouse from a shell company a couple months back.

Armando- Impossible!

Officer Matteo- Isn't this your signature?

Armando- Yes, but Why would I have a warehouse full of cocaine in NY when I am from Chicago.

Officer Matteo- that's what I want to know. Most of the time its illegal activity just like the pallet we found in your warehouse.

Armando- Can I get my phone call?

*(We cut to the call as Matteo exits the building to smoke)*

Armando- Angelo, they fucking played us! Find out what the **Barone's** are up to and get fucking back to me with news! Call our lawyer and get me the fuck out of here.

Angelo- Va bene. (Ok)

*(Matteo is seen on his cell phone)*

Officer Matteo- It's done!

# INT Viva Mexicana Restaurant

Joey- Is Angela here? *(He asks a worker)*

Worker- She's in the back office.

*(He walks to the back office and he sees Angela sitting in the big chair behind her desk)*

Angela- Joey! Dear boy.

Joey- Angela? I want you to leave my family alone!

*(We spot his Gun on his back tucked away in his pants but partially concealed with his shirt)*

Angela- Shhh, have a seat.

*(Joey sits down nervously not expecting what she will do. He stares at her while she stares back with a smile. Joey starts to reach back for his gun)*

Angela- I have not seen you up close in a long time. The last time I saw you, you were a 1 year old baby and I could hold you like this in my arms. *(she mimics rocking a baby)*

*(Joey immediately stops as she makes that reference)*

Joey-What? What are you talk…

*(Angela cuts him off)*

Angela – You have your father's eyes.

Joey- How do you know my father? Who was he?

Angela- You mean who is he?

Joey- He's still alive?

Angela- Well of course he's alive. You see him every day at his café.

Joey- Don is not my biological father.

Angela- But he is..

Joey-Why are you fucking with me right now? *(He starts to reach for the gun again)*

Angela- I'm not? You know why?

Joey- Why is that??

Angela- Because I'm your mother…

Joey- What? No fucking way! Impossible! Don took me in as an orphan.

Angela- He may have took you in but not as an orphan, as his true born son.

Joey- I don't believe you.

Angela- Why do you think you're not dead?

*(Joey thinks for a second with one hand over his head not believing what she is telling him but then he mumbles something to himself)*

Joey- holy shit! Joseph F **Barone**, Felix?

Angela- Yes *(As she smiles)*

Joey- Then why did you shot Frankie!?

Angela- Frankie is not my son. That's Beauty of the business, one son for another. Your father broke a promise to me.

Joey- That makes two of us but Frankie is not the one who killed your son. That's what I came here to tell you… OMG I killed my brother *(He mutters to himself)*

Angela- I have tried to convince your father over and over that he should tell you the truth, but he didn't listen, and because of that Frankie had to pay with his life.

Joey- Frankie is not dead.

Angela- What?! Where is he?

Joey- You really think I'm going to tell you.

Angela-How about this, I'll make a promise here and now that I will never break.

Joey- sure, that makes sense lets even it out. Now that I know, I can be disappointed by both my parents. Go on…

 Angela- I promise to not lay a hair on Frankie's head __IF__ you do something for me.

Joey- What's that?

Angela- Take Daniels place by my side as mother and son and leave the **Barone** name in the wind. Also, you cannot make it known to my daughter Maria that you are my son.

## __INT Maria Beauty Salon__

*(Miquel is on the phone while Maria is in the back office sobbing)*

Miquel- Jesus?

Jesus- ¿Quién es? *(who is this?)*

Miquel- Es miquel, el esposo de Maria. *(Miquel, Maria's husband)*

Jesus- Ahh la contadora. *(Oh the accountant)* Qué pasa *(whats up?)*

Miquel- Tengo que decirte algo. *(I have to tell you something)*

Jesus-seguir *(continue)*

*(Enter Maria few minutes later)*

Maria- Who are you talking to?

*(Miquel holds finger up as to say to Maria one minute, as He walks out to finish the conversation he mentions Jesus's name)*

Miquel- ok, Ciao Jesus

Maria- Jesus! What the fuck have you done Miquel?!

Miquel- Mi Amor, I needed to do this. I cannot have anything happen to you the way it happened to Daniel.

Maria- You just killed us all. You fucking idiot!

*(Maria pushes and hits Miquel toward the door)*

Maria- Get out!

Miquel- I am trying to protect you.

*(Maria pushes him harder toward the exit)*

Maria- Get out now! You better hope my mother doesn't find you before Jesus does!

Miquel- He promised to leave us out of it.

Maria- And you believed him?

*(Miquel grabs Maria holding her tight. Maria struggling to break free knees him in the groin. She quickly runs to her desk and gets a gun from the top draw)*

Maria-Get out now!

*(Miquel with his hands up tries to convince Maria while walking toward her)*

Miquel- Maria no, this is the best thing for both of us. Now we can go wherever we want without your mother holding us back. I love you.

*(Miquel gets closer, while Maria struggles with tears in her eyes)*

Maria- No its not!

Miquel- You're not going to shoot me. You love me.

Maria- Not anymore, you just broke my heart.

*(She shoots, the bullet travels straight through his eye. He falls to the floor. Maria falls to her knees and weeps)*

*(A short time later)*

Luis- Maria, Estas bien?*(are you ok)* Jose will take care of this. Let me take you to your mother.

*(Maria still in shock stares at her dead husband one last time, still with tears in her eyes. She is escorted by Jose to his car and they drive off)*

## <u>INT Angela House</u>

Maria- I'm sorry mother, you were right.

Angela- Don't worry, you did good hija. Go rest

*(Angela Calls Jesus)*

Angela- Hefe?

Jesus- Tu casa no está en orden *(It seems your house is not in order?)*

Angela- Si hefe, He acted alone. Whatever he told you was a lie. I have proof he was skimming money from us for his own personal gain and had to go. He acted in his own best interest.

Jesus- Maya will be sent to oversee all your financials and investigate this matter.

Angela- There is no need, we can take care of it.

Jesus- That was not a question.

*(Hangs up)*

Angela- Fuck!

## <u>INT Viva Mexicana</u>

Angela- This war is over.

Don Gian- Over? I don't believe you Angela.

Angela- Well maybe this will change your mind

*(Angela nods to Jose as Tony and Don stand impatiently waiting what's behind the door. Out walks Joey)*

Don Gian- Joey, che cazzo fai qui! *(What the fuck are you doing here?)*

Angela- He will now be working solely with us. Our partnership is over. You will no longer be moving our product.

*(We cut to the window and see Angelo flick his cigarette bud as he starts to walk away)*

Don Gian- Joey, don't do this. You don't know what she is.

Joey- All I ever wanted was to be a part of this, of the family.

Don Gian- I can make you a part of us. Sempre la familgia remember?

Joey- I don't believe you, Angela was honest with me.

Don Gian- Honest? Honest for selfish reasons. She's a manipulator…

Joey- Io starò con la mia mamma *(I'll stay with my mother)*

Don Gian- *(turns toward Angela)* you told him! That was my responsibility!

Joey- Yes, she told me. Are you going to deny it?

Don Gian- No I am not.

Joey- Then, stay away from me.

Don Gian- So you can stand next to her after what she did to your brother?

Joey- Your lies made me kill my own brother. I can confidently stand next to her knowing nothing further will happen to Frankie.

Don Gian-That's the way it's going to be?

Joey- That's the way it's going to be.

# INT Vincenzo House

Don Gian- I need to talk to my son alone

*(Everyone leaves the room)*

Don Gian- How you feeling?

Frankie- I'm ok what's up? Where's joey?

Don Gian- that's what I came to talk to you about.

Frankie- Is he ok?

Don Gian- He's fine physically.

Frankie- what does that mean? Just tell me what's going on please.

Don Gian- Your brother is now with the Mexican Cartel.

Frankie- What? What are you talking about?

Don Gian- Frankie, Joey is your half-brother. I had him with Angela. She's, his mother.

Frankie- *(Shocked)* You cheated on Mom?! Is that the reason she killed herself?

Don Gian- Si,

Frankie- Do you blame Joey for taking her side? I would too! You couldn't even tell me?!

*(Frankie starts to cough and is starting to gasp for Air. Vincenzo comes in and attends to Frankie)*

Vincenzo- Frankie relax you cannot get all worked up. Relax, try to stay calm.

Frankie- How can I *(coughs)* relax when, *(coughs)* I've been lied to *(coughs)* my whole life.

*(Vincenzo turns to Don)*

Vincenzo- With all due respect Don its best if you let Frankie rest for now.

*(Don gets up and stands a minute before leaving)*

# Chapter 9

# Who I Am

## <u>EXT Calvary Cemetery Woodside NY</u>

*(A priest is saying prayers as Angela, Jose, Luis, Maria and other family members stand with their heads bowed in memory of Daniel. As the casket is being lowered down into the grave site Joey enters and stands beside Angela and Maria. Maria with tears in her eyes whispers to Angela)*

Maria- who is that?

Angela- That's joey he will be working with you and the Joaquin twins on distribution.

Maria- I've seen him enter the café. Isn't he part of the Italian mob?

Angela- No, he is part of our business now.

Maria- We don't work with the Italians anymore?

(Angela shakes her head No)

Angela- Just one.

Maria- Is this because Maya is coming to investigate Miquel's bullshit.

Angela- Partially, keep him away from her.

*(The prayers end and everyone begins walking toward their cars except for Joey, he stays a bit longer. Angela and Maria from afar stop and watch. Joey kneels and extends a flower into the open grave)*

Joey- I wish we had known each other as brothers instead of enemies. They took that from us. They never gave us a chance to understand. My heart is full of anger ,Rage, regret and sorrow. I have been lost my whole life not knowing where I belong. I am trying to figure out who I am and what I need to do. Rest in peace my brother. I am sorry.

## **<u>INT Angela House Memorial Service</u>**

*(Maya walks in with two body guards)*

Angela- Maya! So nice to see you.

Maya- Hola Angela. I'm sorry for your loss.

Angela- Thank you Maya.

Maya- Did you figure out who's responsible?

Angela- It has been taken care of.

Maya- My father told me I would hear that a lot from you.

*(Angela stands visually upset at her comments but reply's back in a calm and respectful demeanor)*

Angela- Can I get you a drink?

Maya- No, I'm fine thank you. I know this is a bad time but I need to get down to business.

Angela- Of course Jose will escort you to the beauty salon, where you can look over all the financials.

Jose- Por favor…

*(Jose puts out is hand and directs Maya and her men toward his car)*

Maya- gracias

*(As Maya walks out of the house Joey catches her eye. She stops and glances for a minute before leaving, Joey notices her as well)*

# **INT Angela House**

*(All guests leave and the immediate family remains. Joey walks up to Maria)*

Joey- Maria, right?

Maria- Yes and you are Joey?

Joey- Yes, it's nice to officially meet you. I wanted to come and give my condolences on the loss of your brother.

Maria- Thank you I appreciate that. So my mother tells me you will be doing a little business with me from now on.

Joey- that's correct. Anything I can help to make your life easier let me know. I'm here for you.

*(Maria confused by Joey's friendliness)*

Maria-thaaaank you, but why are you so eager to help?

Joey- lets just say we have a lot in common.

*(Maria ponders his comments for a moment. All of sudden Maya returns to the house)*

Maria- Excuse me a moment.

*(She walks away)*

Joey- I'll be here if you need anything.

Maria- Hello Maya, it's so nice to meet you I am Angela's daughter, Maria.

Maya- Ah Maria so nice to finally meet you. May I ask you something? Sorry if my English is not perfect.

Maria- Sure,

Maya- Who is that person with blond hair and blue eyes? *(Referring to Joey)*

Maria- He is just a friend of the family.

Maya- Would you mind introducing me?

*(Maria tries to change the subject)*

Maria- he's no one, can I take you to my mother?

Maya- In, a minute.

*(She walks away and toward Joey)*

Maya- Hello, I'm Maya and you are?

Joey- I am Joey.

Maya- How do you know the Felix family?

Joey- I was a very dear friend of Angela's son Daniel. How do you know Angela?

*(Maria stands close and to overhear the conversation)*

Maya- I'm sorry for the loss of your friend. We are close business associates.

Joey- I see.

Maya- I will be here for a couple days. Maybe we can get a cup of coffee to better get to know each other.

Joey- Sure I would like that.

Maya- Here's my hotel number, call me anytime.

*(Maria notices the sexual tension and Interrupts)*

Maria- Maya my mother is ready to see you. Follow me this way.

Joey- Pleasure.

Maya- It was all mine.

*(She walks to Angela's office with Maria)*

Angela- Maya, back so soon?

Maya- I'm good at what I do.

Angela- so?

Maya- it seems your claims are correct he was skimming money. His death was justifiable; however I need to know more about this company, ITMC.

Angela- That's just a shell company we use for our distribution.

Maya- My father would like to know more about the people you are working with since you no longer employee the Joaquin twins for the west coast.

Angela- Actually we will be using them from this point forward.

Maya- that's unfortunate, however I was sent here to look up previous financials not the current. It says the company exits here in NY.

Angela- Sure, why don't you go relax at the hotel from your long flight and we will gather the information and provided for you tomorrow.

Maya- I could use a drink.

Angela- sure, Luis!

Luis- Si?

Angela- What do you drink?

Maya- Thanks but I'd rather have a drink at the hotel bar, no disrespect intended.

Angela-None taken, Luis will escort you and your associates.

Maya- ok hasta mañana.

*(They leave and Maria and Angela have a conversation)*

Maria- we have a problem

## **INT FBI Headquarters Manhattan**

Detective Morrow- Gian **Barone**. Nice to meet you. Thank you for coming down.

Don Gian- Pleasure, this is my lawyer Silvestro Pinto.

*(They all greet each other with handshakes)*

Detective Morrow- It seems like quite a mess you created at your residents.

Silvestro - I'm sorry are you accusing my client of something? He willfully came down here to speak to you.

Detective Morrow- I'm not accusing him of anything I just need to know the facts of that night

Don Gian- I was not home the night of the shooting. I was in my place of business at Café di Napoli.

Detective Morrow- Do you have anyone that can verify?

Silvestro - We can do you one better. We have surveillance that Mr **Barone** was in fact in Café di Napoli at around the time of the shooting.

Detective  Morrow- Nice Alibi.. However, we found some blood

Silvestro - Was it matched to my client?

Detective Morrow- No, it was covered in bleach

(Silvestro *starts to speak when Don stops and interrupts him*)

Don Gian- Norrow right?

Detective Morrow- Morrow actually… *(Seemingly annoyed)*

Don Gian- ok Norrow, as you can see in the camera footage, I was at my place of business on the night of the shooting. What more proof do you need?

Detective Morrow- Yes, I see that however since this was at your place of residence you can see why I would need to ask you further questions regarding what occurred the night of the shootings? Do you have anyone who would want to harm you or your family?

Don Gian- I am a legitimate businessman. Name one businessman who has not made enemies along the way?

Detective Morrow- Well that's what I am trying to figure out. We came across a lot of dead bodies

Silvestro  Is my client under arrest here?

Detective  Morrow- No, not yet.

Silvestro - well if you have no evidence, we will be on our way.

Detective Morrow- Don't go too far, you never know what new evidence might surface.

(*As they begin to walk out another detective enters the room*)

Lorenzo Belli- Detective Morrow?

Detective Morrow- Yes?

Lorenzo- FBI agent Alex Lorenzo, I need all your documents related  to the **Barone** resident's crime scene.

Detective Morrow- Why?

Lorenzo Belli - We have reason to believe this was a Mexican gang related incident that spilled onto the **Barone** residence.

*(Don having overheard turns toward Detective Morrow and displays a minor smirk on his face)*

Detective Morrow- I would like to interrogate them.

Lorenzo Belli - You have no jurisdiction on this matter

*(Detective Morrow stands there visibly upset handing over the evidence)*

## **INT Prison Visitation**

*(Armando is escorted in the visitor's room and we see Angelo sitting on the other side of the glass. He sits and they both pick up the phone)*

Armando – well?

Angelo- ho trovato qualcosa. *(i found something)*

*(Once the conversation is done Armando is being taken back to his cell when he asks the guard something)*

Armando- I want my phone call now. Do these phones make international calls?

# <u>INT Warehouse Astoria</u>

*(Joey and Maria are having a conversation)*

Maria- You used to hang out in front of café Di Napoli no? Why change corners?

Joey- Creative differences.

Maria- what do you mean by that?

Joey- Let's just say that your mothers helping me grow.

Maria- Why do I feel like you and my mother are not being totally honest with me?

Joey- the feelings mutual.

*(Enter the Joaquin twins)*

Maria- Santiago, Xavier, long time

Santiago Joaquin - Maria Esta bene? *(Are you good?)*

Maria- Si, grazies.

Xavier Joaquin - Hola Maria, I'm sorry to hear about Daniel. My condolences.

Santiago- Si, my condolences.

Maria- Grazies mucho, this is Joey. He will be working with me in place of Daniel.

Santiago- Un poco blanco no? *(A Little White, no?)*

Joey- Blanca solo a través de la piel *(white only through skin)*

*(Maria is taken back that Joey knows Spanish)*

Xavier-*(laughs)* chico gracioso *(haha funny guy)* nice to meet you.

*(They shake hands)*

Joey- 4 años de español de secundaria. *(4 years of high school Spanish)*

Santiago- Muy bueno, you have a nice accent as well.

Maria- Now that we've all been introduced, let me show you the product, this way please.

*(As they walk Xavier strikes up a conversation with Joey)*

Xavier- So Joey where are you from?

Joey- Queens

Xavier- No I mean heritage wise.

Joey- I was adopted so I don't really know.

*(Maria sees how careful Joey is being and seems impressed)*

Maria—Here, 100 kilos.

Santiago- bene, the price still the same?

Maria- 10% Bump.

Santiago- steep price Maria, how come?

Maria- let's just say the people who moved it for us before paid more than this.

Santiago- I can't take a significate loss and as I can tell you have no channels of distribution at the moment. So you have to work with me here.

Maria- That's the best I can do.

Santiago- I'm sorry, then we can't do business. Vamos Xavier.

Joey- Wait! Why don't we do something here?

Santiago- what do you have in mind, blanco?

Joey- You take the first two shipments 200 Kilo's in total, 5% Less than you used to pay to build up your profit margin.

Maria- Joey!

Joey- Hold on; after the first two you pay our price and we will even throw in an extra Quarter Kilo for personal use?

Xavier- Half a Kilo…

Joey- Done deal.

*(They shake hands)*

Xavier- I fucking like this guy.

Joey- We will be in touch.

*(The Joaquin twins load the truck and leave)*

Joey- We need them.

Maria- You didn't have the authority to do that; however, I can say I am very impressed with you thus far.

*(Maria tries to kiss Joey to where he immediately backs off)*

Joey- Ew, what are you doing?

Maria- Ew?? What are you gay?

Joey- No I'm not.

Maria- Then what? I put myself out there and..

Joey- *(joey stutters a moment)*, uh sorry I was just taken by surprise that's all.
I don't really like to mix business with pleasure.

*(Annoyed, Maria begins suspecting something)*

Maria- Lets just go.

## **EXT Josephine's Bar Manhattan**

*(Frankie and Tony pull up to a bar in Manhattan called Josephine's bar)*

Frankie-Josephine's Bar?

*(They proceed into the back and down some stairs into a basement where we see a fully furnished apartment and Don is sitting awaiting for Frankie)*

Frankie- Something else I was kept in the dark from huh?

Don Gian- Frankie, Sit down.

*(Helped by Tony, Frankie sits down)*

Don Gian- I opened this up after your mother passed away. It's all legitimate. This is something to fall back on if things go bad.

Frankie- All worked out well wouldn't you say? Joey is running with the enemy.

Don Gian- I'm sorry I lied to you and your brother. I wish I could take it back but It was the only way I could keep you safe. If we want any hope of things working out, you have to go talk to your brother

Frankie- Don't you think you should?

Don Gian- He will only listen to you.

# INT Joey's Apartment

*(Joey enters the apartment and to his surprise he sees Frankie sitting waiting for him)*

Joey- Frankie? What are you doing here? How are you feeling?

Frankie- good, I can finally move by myself.

Joey- I'm happy you are ok but you should not be here.

Frankie- I came to talk some sense into you.

Joey- You should leave.

Frankie- No, not until we talk this out. You're a part of our family not theirs.

Joey- It seems I am tied into both families or did he not tell you?

Frankie- He told me and I was just as upset for you as I was for me.

Joey- It doesn't matter anymore.

Frankie- Joey we are brothers! You know how many times you wished it were true.

Joey- but so much has changed. I at least understand who I am on this side of the street. I never knew who I was on yours. I love you guys but this is the best way to protect you.

Frankie- I know who you are joey…. You're a **Barone**! I hope you realize it before it's too late.

*(We don't hear the rest of their conversation but Frankie leaves and we notice Luis watching from the car, all of a sudden Tony sneaks up to the open window and he raps a cord around his neck and slowly chocks him to death. Maria sees this all play out as she had followed Joey to his apartment in a separate vehicle, and she takes off.)*

# <u>Ext Cafe Di Napoli</u>

*(Tony and Gino are having an expresso outside café di Napoli when a car starts to drive real slowly passed the café all of sudden the windows open and shots reign out. Tony and Gino try to take cover but Gino is shot three times in the chest where Tony takes one on the shoulder, he tries to shoot back but the car peels off)*

# <u>INT Marriott Hotel Bar</u>

Joey- Hello Maya,

Maya- Joey thanks for coming. I really needed a drink and hate drinking alone.

Joey- let me call that guy over to keep you company.

Maya- you're funny.

Joey- so, what do I owe this pleasure?

Maya- I just wanted to get to know you a little better while I'm in town

Joey- So this has nothing to do with the fact that you find me attractive?

Maya- Maybe a little.

*(They both smile and Joey tries to get the bartenders attention)*

Joey- Can I get an amaretto on the rocks and whatever the lady is drinking

Maya- Bloody Mary thanks.

Bartender- I'll be right back with those drinks for you.

Joey- Bloody Mary huh? I hope it's not that time of month.

Maya- No I just like things bloody *(she gives Joey a look)*

Joey- So what else am I really here for? because you like me or are you trying to gather some Intel on the Felix's?

Maya- Would you be mad if I said a little bit of both?

Joey- Not at all, I am in a giving kind of mood.

# Chapter 10

## *'They Know'*

### <u>INT Vincenzo's House</u>

*(Tony on the phone and in pain)*

Tony- Don, don

Don Gian- Tony, what's the matter?

Tony- They got Gino, Gino.

Don Gian- fuck! You ok?

Tony- Just a little flesh wound, Vincenzo's patching me up, up. What do you want to do, do?

Don Gian- chiama le famiglie. *(Call the families)*

### <u>INT Josephine's Bar</u>

*(Tony arrives with his arm in a sling to meet frankie and Don)*

Don Gian- Well?

Tony-*(shakes his head no)* I call Ranile, and no answer, answer

*(We cut to see Vinny Ranile's body hit the floor, blood everywhere)*

Tony- I call lentucci and no answer, answer

*(We cut to see Joe Lentucci's body hit the floor)*

Don Gian- I try johnny now to see if he knows anything

*(Phone rings for about 15 seconds all of sudden someone picks up and phone is on speaker with no voice on the other end)*

Don Gian- Johnny?

Johnny- *(In a panic)* Don!

Don Gian- Johnny, what's going on you ok?

Sylvester Scopa- hai fatto una cazzata. *(You fucked up)*

*(You hear a shot and phone hangs up)*

Don Gian- Figlio di puttana, NO!!!

Frankie- what happened?

Don Gian- They know! Those Sons of bitches know!

Frankie- who knows?

Don Gian- The Scopa's, Sylvester just killed Johnny

## __INT Marriott Hotel__

*(Joey and Maya wake up from a passionate night of love making)*

Maya- I wouldn't mind waking up to your face, between my legs.

Joey- ok we'll play Titanic. You'll be the iceberg and ill be the ship.

*(Joeys phone rings)*

Joey- fuck… hello Yah?

Maria- My mother would like to see you.

Joey- ok I'm on my way.

*(Hangs Up)*

Joey- I gotta go.

Maya- Be careful.

*(They embrace in a kiss and Joey leaves)*

## **INT Prison**

*(Armando walks out to the visitors room and to his pleasant surprise he sees Don sitting behind the glass waiting. He excerpts an evil smile on his face)*

Armando- the great Don Gian!

Don Gian- You want the truth??

Armando- That's all I ever wanted from you.Don Gian- Then you have to do something for me.

## **INT Viva Mexicana**

Joey- Ángela?

Angela- Have a seat Joey.

Joey- What's going on?

Angela- so you're not going to tell me?

Joey- Tell you what?

Angela- That your brother Frankie came to your apartment.

Maria- Brother?

Angela- Yes Joey and Frankie are brothers.

Joey- I wanted to see how he was doing after your men shot him and almost killed him.

Angela- You disappoint me.

*(Jose punches him in the face)*

Maria- what are you doing? This is not what we talked about.

*(Jose punches him again)*

Angela- He deserves this. He killed your brother.

*(Maria is in shock)*

Maria- what?

Angela- Yes he killed Daniel. He was sleeping with Veronica.

Maria- why didn't you tell me? *(Angrily)*

*(Angela ignores her daughter)*

Angela- You think you can outsmart me huh? Sleeping with Maya and telling her everything?

Joey- what the fuck did you do? *(spits out blood)*

*(We see Maya's guards get brutally murdered and Maya kidnapped and thrown into a truck)*

Angela- She still alive, for now.

Maria- Mother why? That's Jesus daughter.

Angela- don't worry about Jesus, he will be next.

Joey- Fuck you Mother!

*(Jose punches joey a couple more times)*

Maria- Mother? What the fuck is going on?!

Joey- Oh that's right she didn't tell you huh? I'm your brother. Why you think I didn't kiss you?

Angela- Kiss him?! What? He's lying to you Hija.

Joey- Is this a lie?!

*(He pulls out a paper and shows Maria a birth certificate with Don Gian and Angela's name on it)*

Joey- That's right Frankie brought me the proof to show your daughter! You lying cunt! They are more a family to me then you'll ever be!

*(Jose punches Joey a few more times)*

Maria- Stop it!

Joey- She never told you the whole story huh Maria? How she knew the whole time about me and Veronica and even went as far as ripping her finger nails off. Daniel is dead because your mother lied to you. I wish I had known earlier, I would have put a bullet in her head instead of Daniel.

*(Angela gets up and back slaps Joey a few times herself; Joey spits the blood back in her face)*

Joey- fuck you!

Angela- I should have let **Eduardo** kill you when you were baby. Get him out of my sight!

Maria- My father knew? Daniel was right he didn't die in a car accident you killed him didn't you?

Angela- I did what I had to do.

Maria- You're fucking crazy!

Angela- Are you with me or with them? I'd choose wisely my daughter.

Maria-(*She pauses a moment*) I can't forgive him for killing Daniel, I'm with you.

Angela- Smart choose.

Maria- what are you going to do to him?

Angela- Bait!

# Chapter 11

# "Pensa Sempre A La Famiglia" ("Think Always Of The Family")

## <u>Astoria Warehouse</u>

*(Don, Frankie and Tony are all stopped at the front door of the warehouse by Jose who proceeds to pat them down for any weapons, while other members of the cartel stand by)*

Frankie- I don't think my dick can be used as a weapon! Asshole!

*(Jose Gives Frankie a look and proceeds to let them in)*

Angela- Welcome!

*(We see Joey and Maya hands tied, sitting side by side. Joey has noticeable bruises on his face)*

Don Gian- What the fuck did you do to him? He's your fucking son Angela!

Angela- Both my sons died a long time ago.

Frankie- Aren't we here to talk? That shit is uncalled for!

Maria- Joey killing Daniel was uncalled for.

Don Gian- Everyone, relax! Angela how do we get passed this?

Angela- I don't think there is a way to get past this. He not only disobeyed me by seeing Frankie after I told him not to, he also tried to reason with my bosses' daughter to get rid of me. Does that sound like a son to you?

Frankie- Maybe he had a legitimate reason to do so.

Angela- Shut the fuck up you. You should have died in your house that night!

Don Gian- Calma… (*Calm down),* so why accept this meeting here today?

Angela- so you can watch him die!

*(Angela nods to Maria she pulls out her gun and points it at Joey head)*

Frankie- Maria, please don't!

Maria- You took my brother away from me and Lied to my face.

*(She Turns and points the gun at Angela)*

Angela- What are you doing?

Maria- You killed my father, you killed Veronica and you are the reason my brother and my husband are dead! You are the devil.

*(Jose takes out his gun and points it at Marias head)*

Jose- Drop it Maria. Now!

Maria- I can't do that Jose, I am not losing another brother. You're going to have to shoot me.

*(Suddenly shots reign out, a couple cartel members are shot dead and Jose is shot in the shoulder. He drops his gun as bullets continue to fly around them. They all take cover as Joey jumps with his body and tackles Maya to the ground to avoid the flood of bullets. Angela proceeds to take out a weapon and has a clear shot at Joey. Tony seeing this jumps right in the line of fire and is shot)*

Joey- NOOOO!

*(Angela then notices Maria and wants to make her pay for what she has just done. She shoots and Frankie tackles her away and again gets shot, this time in the leg. Frankie*

*finds a gun on the floor; he turns and shoots a few times at Jose killing him instantly. At this point all who are left standing are Don, Joey, Maya, Maria and Angela, while Frankie sits shot in the leg)*

Angelo Bimino- everyone ok? Sit the fuck down you *(pointing his Gun at Angela)* DROP IT!

*(Angela proceeds to drop her gun)*

Sal Domini- Frankie you ok?

Frankie- Yah but I'm tired of getting shot.

*(We see Joey by Tonys side as he is struggling to breath. Frankie hobbles to his side as well)*

Joey- T, T! I'm sorry T I'm sorry

*(Tony manages to get one last sentence in before he dies)*

Tony- pensa sempre a la famiglia. Fam..

*(He takes his last breath and passes away)*

Frankie- T, NO!

*(Both Frankie and Joey are crying while Don is standing in noticeable pain to the loss of his best friend. He picks up a gun and walks toward Angela)*

Don Gian- You love when I speak in Italian to you right? vai all'inferno *(Go to hell!)*

*(Bang!)*

Angelo- Everyone ok? *(Unties Joey and Maya)*

Don Gian- Si Grazie, Angelo.

Angelo- My pleasure Zio… *(Smiles)* I always believed you loved my aunt, you know.

Don Gian- I still do.

*(Maria walks up to Frankie)*

Maria- Thank you.

*(She kisses him)*

*(Maya hugs Joey to comfort him on the loss of Tony)*

Maya- I'm sorry Joey.

Sal Domini- I'm Sorry about Tony, Joe.

Joey- Thanks, thanks for coming through for us

Sal- I'm here whenever you need me brother!

*(They slap hands and embrace in a hug)*

## <u>EXT WOODSIDE, MASPETH Calvary Cemetery</u>

*(The priest is saying prayers as family members stand with their heads bowed in memory of Tony. Before the casket is lowered into the grave site Joey has a few things to say)*

Joey- It was hard to see at first how full your heart was with love. I see now once it's too late how much we meant to you and how much you mean to us. You were not family in blood but family nonetheless. You gave me not one but two chances at life that I can never repay. I'm sorry my heart was not full of love back then, but it is full of love now. You will forever be engraved in my heart until the day we meet again. Pensa Sempre la famiglia. I love you T! *(As tears fall from his eyes)*

Frankie- We love you T, Sempre! *(Always)*

*(They all head out except for Don who stays for a private moment)*

Don Gian- You were the greatest friend I could ever have asked for. You protected my boys like they were yours and I am forever grateful.  We will meet again very soon my friend.

## INT Dons House Memorial Service For Tony

*(Everyone is sitting telling stories about Tony. We see Frankie with Maria, Joey with Maya, Sal and other family members around when Sylvester scopa comes through the door and nods at Don. He puts up his finger to signal one minute where he calls Joey and Frankie to come into the other room)*

Joey- What's going on?

Frankie- Yah what's up? We were reminiscing of a story Tony told me about his trip to Chicago.

Don Gian- Come here, both of you. Give me a hug.

*(They all embrace in a hug)*

Joey- Are you ok Papa?

Don Gian-I need you both to stick together no matter what.

Frankie- why are you saying this?

Don Gian- I have a date with destiny.

Joey- Is she hot?

*(Don laughs)*

Don Gian- I'm gona miss you, you sarcastic little prick. The bimino family didn't help us out from the kindness of their hearts. I need to give them something in return.

Frankie- Give them what?

Don Gian – Control of the 5 families.

Joey- Its ok, you can retire and be at my wedding. *(He smiles)* Im getting married.

Don Gian- Congratulations! I'm happy for you Figlio Mio

Joey- I am also going back to college while Maya handles the distribution for her father here in the states.

Don Gian-*(smiles)* I can't stay. I wish I could.

Frankie- what you mean? You can't stay?

Don Gian- Part of the deal was I have to give myself over to Scopa family and return to Napoli for the family crimes I committed.

Joey-No! I won't let that happen!

Frankie- Fuck that! Let them come!

Don Gian-This needs to be done to guarantee the safety of you boys and I will do it over and over again if I had to. The Café and Laundry matt have been sold. The money is in these accounts for you boys *(hands them overseas bank books)*. Frankie, watch over your mother's bar for me.

*(They all begin to shed a tear and embrace in one more long-lasting hug, knowing that their father will never return)*

Don Gian- I love you boys. Pensa sempre la Famiglia!

Frankie/Joey- Pensa sempre la Famiglia!

*(They leave the room and Sylvester Scopa escorts don into a vehicle as Frankie and Joey watch from the window with tears in their eyes)*

Don Gian- Can we make one stop before the airport.

*(Sylvester nods his head yes as Don waves to his boys one last time. A few minutes after they leave Detective Morrow arrives)*

Detective Morrow- Is your father home?

Frankie- No, he is out.

Detective Morrow- Can you please tell him to come down to the precinct ASAP, we have some questions for him regarding the shooting at the Café.

*(Frankie and Joey smile for a brief second)*

Frankie-As soon as he gets back I will let him know.

## **EXT WOODSIDE, MASPETH Calvary Cemetery**

*(Don and Sylvester walk to a grave site that reads Josephine Bimino Barone, loving mother and worlds best Wife. He kneels in front of the stone)*

Don Gian- I'm sorry it's been more than 15 years that I have not come to visit you. I was scared; scared that you would never forgive me for what I did even after you left this earth. He may not have been yours, but he was damn well important for me to fight for. I wish you would have just given it a chance because I still loved you. I do still love you and I will see you real soon, Mio Amore.

*(As don is about to get up a flower blows towards him and lands right on his lap. He smiles and we fade out)*

*The End!*

117